THE GRAYWOLF RE/VIEW SERIES, EDITED BY MARK DOTY

Lynda Hull (1954–1994) was perhaps the most intensely lyrical poet of her generation. Her charged, sensuous music—influenced by jazz and the densely wrought sonics of Hart Crane—is wedded to an indelible vision. In her broken, late-century American landscape of ruined cities, a desparate beauty flashes among the wreckage of individual lives. This volume gathers together her three collections—long unavailable—with a new introduction by Yusef Komunyakaa, and allows, for the first time, the full scale of her achievement to be seen.

The Graywolf Re/View Series brings essential books of contemporary American poetry back into the light of print. Each volume—chosen by series editor Mark Doty—is introduced by a poet who comes to the work with a passionate admiration. The Graywolf Re/View Series offers all-but-lost masterworks of recent American poetry to a new generation of readers.

Forthcoming volumes in the Graywolf Re/View series:
Thomas James, introduced by Lucie Brock-Broido
James L. White, introduced by Mark Doty

Books by Lynda Hull

The Only World
Star Ledger
Ghost Money

Lynda Hull
Collected Poems

Graywolf Press
SAINT PAUL, MINNESOTA

Publication of this volume is made possible in part by a grant provided by the Minnesota State Arts Board, through an appropriation by the Minnesota State Legislature; a grant from the Wells Fargo Foundation Minnesota; and a grant from the National Endowment for the Arts, which believes that a great nation deserves great art. Significant support has also been provided by the Bush Foundation; Target; the McKnight Foundation; and other generous contributions from foundations, corporations, and individuals. To these organizations and individuals we offer our heartfelt thanks.

MINNESOTA
STATE ARTS BOARD

NATIONAL
ENDOWMENT
FOR THE ARTS

Ghost Money was originally published by the University of Massachusetts Press, 1986.
Star Ledger was originally published by the University of Iowa Press, 1991.
The Only World was originally published by HarperCollins, 1995.

Published by Graywolf Press
2402 University Avenue, Suite 203
Saint Paul, Minnesota 55114

www.graywolfpress.org

Published in the United States of America

ISBN-13 978-1-55597-457-2
ISBN-10 1-55597-457-0

2 4 6 8 9 7 5 3 1

First Graywolf Printing, 2006

Library of Congress Control Number: 2006924338

Cover design: Kyle G. Hunter
Cover photograph: Michael Trombley

Contents

Three

Introduction

A radical simplicity throbs in the central nervous system of Lynda Hull's poignant vision. In her poetry each word seems informed by need, and every gesture has been refined and shaped by passion and deft precision. Since her first collection, *Ghost Money*, was published in 1986, Hull's work has beckoned to those who embrace a poetry that can matter in their daily lives. There's always a mystique that encapsulates those artists who die young, but there's a taunting question surrounding Lynda Hull: since her early work is so brilliant, what would time have given us? To use an old jazz phrase: she had the chops to accomplish anything she wanted to do in her poetry. Indeed, she reminds me of a few of those jazz greats who died prematurely and left us a legacy. I think Lynda would welcome this comparison, especially since she composed such heartrending portraits of musicians. She also shows how the music seethed into the lives of those around her, how it crossed so many borders to establish a resonance true to mind and flesh; and to see this illustrated in all its brilliance and lyrical exactitude, one only has to read the first two stanzas of "The Charmed Hour":

On the radio, gypsy jazz. Django Reinhardt
    puts a slow fire to Ellington's *Solitude*
        while ice cubes pop in your martini. The sting
of lime on my palm. By the sink you lean,
    twisting your rings. Turn to the window.

In shadow you could be sixteen
    again, in your mother's kitchen

above Cleveland, the cafés of Warsaw still
smoky in your mind with talk and cigarettes,
    English still a raw mystery of verbs.

Music provides this poet with the space in which she addresses
the vagaries of personal and public histories. It binds everything
and codifies a continuity in her quest for a beautiful, biting clar-
ity. At times, however, a line of hers may make one think of a
straight razor wrapped in silk cloth. Again and again, her urbane
wit surprises and cuts deeply.

Yes, for anyone who truly loves poetry, who's willing to em-
brace everything it reveals, and who believes in and trusts this
risky enterprise that attempts to make us whole, I feel that he
or she would agree that Lynda Hull is a great voice among us.
She possessed the genius of synthesis, how to make seemingly
disparate worlds interweave and live side-by-side in the same
poem, with a syncopated silence resounding and threading it all
together. Also, she possessed a sense of emotional history that
at times seems burdensome; and in that sense, "1933" is a living
skein woven of aching language—not a conclusion foretold, but
a moment of revelation. After reading Lynda's poetry for over
twenty years, I still feel that "1933" is a pivotal poem, that its tone
instructs me how to hear the body of her work:

    Whole countries hover, oblivious on the edge
    of history and in Cleveland the lake
    already is dying. None of this matters
    to my mother at seven, awakened from sleep

    to follow her father through darkened rooms
    downstairs to the restaurant emptied
    of customers, chairs stacked and steam glazing
    the window, through the kitchen bright with pans,

ropes of kielbasa, the tubs of creamy lard
that resemble, she thinks, ice cream.
At the tavern table her father's friends
talk rapidly to a man in a long gray coat,

in staccato French, Polish, harsh German.
Her mother stops her, holds her shoulders, and whispers
This is a famous man. Remember his face.
Trotsky—a name like one of her mother's

fond, strange nouns. He looks like the man
who makes her laugh at Sunday matinées,
only tired. So tired. Her father pours the man
another drink of clear, bootleg gin, then turns

smiling to her. She has her own glass.
Peppermint schnapps that burns and makes her light,
cloudy so grown-ups forget her when she curls
on a bench and drifts then wakes and drifts again.

These first six of seventeen stanzas are stated rather matter-of-factly, embodying a tone of personal lore and familiarity, as if the speaker has been gifted with an immense history that transverses various way stations of the heart. The story's told with great simplicity. The poem ends this way:

The men who wait each night
outside the kitchen door have a look she's seen
in her father's eyes, although it's two years
until he turns his gentle hand against himself.

But now he touches her face. Her father stands
so straight, as if wearing a uniform he's proud of.

She watches him shape the sign of the cross.
She crosses forehead, lips, and breast, and believes,

for a moment, her father could cradle the world
in his palm. When they leave the church and its flickering
votive candles for market, it is dawn. The milkman's
wagon horse waits, patient at the curb, his breath

rosettes of steam rising to the sky that spills
like a pail of blue milk across morning. She prays
that God take care of the man in the gray coat,
that her father will live forever.

Hull's poetry creates tension through what the reader believes
he or she knows; it juxtaposes moments that allude to public his-
tory alongside private knowledge. Thus, each poem challenges and
coaxes the reader into an act of participation.

As we journey through Hull's three collections, *Ghost Money*,
Star Ledger, and *The Only World*, we learn how the love-strategy
of jazz functions in this poet's work, how a mere reference or
name can often turn into something new that surprises us. The
flow in her poetry always seems natural—as if secrets are being
whispered only for our ears. All the references to music and musi-
cians, to a cacophony of phrases and needful silences, everything
echoes and pulls us back to the source, to what really matters in
this world. Oftentimes, her poetry embraces risks, with a gutsy
signifier in the driver's seat, which comes through so clearly as we
arrive at those two words which momentarily shocks us into an
intellectual and emotional stance in "Lost Fugue for Chet": "Fuck
Death." One realizes that this isn't insensitivity or bravado, but it
underlines a failed moment in communication with the Self. It is
like a desperate screech through a jazz musician's trumpet or sax.
At first, "Fuck Death" may seem inappropriate; but on second or

third thought, one realizes that this poet perfected a language that speaks to the mind and the body through measured skill and wit.

When we attempt to measure the loss of Lynda Hull, we may appear selfish and greedy, questing after those poems silenced by her untimely death in 1994. Our what-ifs may cloud the painful air. But now, finally, after lengthy anticipation, we can hold this wonderful body of work in our hands. Lynda Hull's *Collected Poems* assures us that we can now luxuriate in what many of us already knew: our friend, Lynda, is truly a marvelous poet. Always uniquely herself, she's ours to behold and cherish through the decades.

Yusef Komunyakaa

Ghost Money

"White, through white cities passed on to
 assume that world which comes to each of us
alone."

> *Hart Crane*

"And all things are forgiven . . . it would be
 strange not to forgive."

> *Anton Chekhov*

Spell for the Manufacture & Use of a Magic Carpet

When the last commuter trains etch
black signatures of departure over tracks
and subways glide untroubled through quiet tunnels,
find an obscure girl. Let her weave a carpet
of white & new wool, the best wool

of the Garment District. Obtain a wand
from the Armenian in the hour of the sun
when the moon is full & in Capricorn. Go to a park
or a rooftop where you'll suffer no disturbance.
Spread your carpet facing East & West,

& having drawn a circle to enclose it,
hold your wand in the air. Name backward
the chain of names from each current of the past into
whatever crests foamless toward the future.
Invoke the faces abandoned in cloakrooms

of childhood, summoning each discarded
voice. Thank each panicked corridor & lucid
clinic doorway, blessing the hands that ministered
to you for they have carried you to this
wild incompletion. Remember them,

shed them in the East & North,
to the South & West, raising in turn each
of the carpet's corners. Go home. Fold your carpet
until you need it. Order your house
& remove each dooryard stone.

Wait for a night of full or new moon
when open windows free the sleepers' heated breath.
On a roof where you'll risk no harm, write with a feather,
on a strip of azure parchment, those characters
found on page three hundred and seven

in the Dictionary of Angels. Hold
the wand in your left hand, the parchment
in your right, recite the arcana of angels for each
precinct. Thank whatever god you understand,
whatever buoys you past

each harbored absence. Ask then
to discover the secret thing you seek,
gazing out always over the diners & arcades
to the cities of New Jersey rising
white, small beyond the Palisades.

ONE

Tide of Voices

At the hour the streetlights come on, buildings
turn abstract. The Hudson, for a moment, formal.
We drink bourbon on the terrace and you speak
in the evening voice, weighted deep in the throat.

They plan to harvest oysters, you tell me,
from the harbor by Jersey City, how the waters
will be clean again in twenty years. I imagine nets
burdened with rough shells, the meat dun and sexual.

Below, the river and the high rock
where boys each year jump from bravado
or desperation. The day flares, turns into itself.
And innocently, sideways, the way we always fall

into grace or knowledge, we watched the police
drag the river for a suicide, the third this year.
The terrible hook, the boy's frail whiteness.
His face was blank and new as your face

in the morning before the day has worked
its pattern of lines and tensions. A hook
like an iron question and this coming
out of the waters, a flawed pearl —

a memory that wasn't ours to claim.
Perhaps, in a bedroom by lamplight,
a woman waits for this boy. She may riffle drawers
gathering photographs, string, keys to abandoned rooms.

Even now she may be leaving,
closing the door for some silence. I need
to move next to you. Water sluiced
from the boy's hair. I need to watch you

light your cigarette, the flickering
of your face in matchlight, as if underwater,
drifting away. I take your cigarette
and drag from it, touch your hand.

Remember that winter of your long fever,
the winter we understood how fragile
any being together was. The wall sweated
behind the headboard and you said you felt

the rim where dreams crouch
and every room of the past. It must begin in luxury —
do you think—a break and fall into the glamour
attending each kind of surrender. Water must flood

the mind, as in certain diseases, the walls
between the cells of memory dissolve, blur
into a single stream of voices and faces.
I don't know any more about this river or if

it can be cleaned of its tender and broken histories—
a tide of voices. And this is how the dead
rise to us, transformed: wet and singing,
the tide of voices pearling in our hands.

Insect Life of Florida

In those days I thought their endless thrum
    was the great wheel that turned the days, the nights.
       In the throats of hibiscus and oleander

I'd see them clustered yellow, blue, their shells
    enameled hard as the sky before rain.
       All that summer, my second, from city

to city my young father drove the black coupe
    through humid mornings I'd wake to like fever
       parceled between luggage and sample goods.

Afternoons, showers drummed the roof,
    my parents silent for hours. Even then I knew
       something of love was cruel, was distant.

Mother leaned over the seat to me, the orchid
    Father'd pinned in her hair shriveled
       to a purple fist. A necklace of shells

coiled her throat, moving a little as she
    murmured of alligators that float the rivers
       able to swallow a child whole, of mosquitoes

whose bite would make you sleep a thousand years.
    And always the trance of blacktop shimmering
       through swamps with names like incantations—

Okeefenokee, where Father held my hand
    and pointed to an egret's flight unfolding
       white above swamp reeds that sang with insects

until I was lost, until I was part
      of the singing, their thousand wings gauze
         on my body, tattooing my skin.

Father rocked me later by the water,
      on the motel balcony, singing calypso
         above the Jamaican radio. The lyrics

a net over the sea, its lesson
      of desire and repetition. Lizards flashed
         over his shoes, over the rail

where the citronella burned, merging our
      shadows—Father's face floating over mine
         in the black changing sound

of night, the enormous Florida night,
      metallic with cicadas, musical
         and dangerous as the human heart.

The Fitting

The room smelled of steam
the day my tall sad mother
brought me to watch
the fitting. Heat knocked
old pipes below the window
where I sat, cheek cradled
on the pane, elbow
pushed among violets
and cactus crowding the sill.
Murmuring of patterns,
the women unfolded damask
my father had brought
from Turkey, almost
too heavy for the afternoon.
The seamstress frightened me,
her hands discovering
my mother's shape
as she hummed
through the pins in her mouth.
I watched until
my head ached
and felt thin as glass.
In the sky
wind milled clouds, promised
no animals or countries.
Only seamless gray.
My tongue was difficult,
sullen as the buildings
repeating a red-brick phrase
down the street.
I pricked my finger

on the cactus—said nothing,
hearing the silence
in the room. Then, I saw
my mother step toward me
changing the air.
In the dimness,
I touched my hair,
the same soft hair
that aureoled her face.
A bright drop welled
on my finger, and everywhere,
the scent of violets, steam.

1933

Whole countries hover, oblivious on the edge
of history and in Cleveland the lake
already is dying. None of this matters
to my mother at seven, awakened from sleep

to follow her father through darkened rooms
downstairs to the restaurant emptied
of customers, chairs stacked and steam glazing
the window, through the kitchen bright with pans,

ropes of kielbasa, the tubs of creamy lard
that resemble, she thinks, ice cream.
At the tavern table her father's friends
talk rapidly to a man in a long gray coat,

in staccato French, Polish, harsh German.
Her mother stops her, holds her shoulders, and whispers
This is a famous man. Remember his face.
Trotsky—a name like one of her mother's

fond, strange nouns. He looks like the man
who makes her laugh at Saturday matinées,
only tired. So tired. Her father pours the man
another drink of clear, bootleg gin, then turns

smiling to her. She has her own glass.
Peppermint schnapps that burns and makes her light,
cloudy so grown-ups forget her when she curls
on a bench and drifts then wakes and drifts again.

At the bar, her mother frowns, braids shining
round her head bent to the books, the columns
of figures in her bold hand and the smoke, voices
of men, a wash of syllables she sleeps upon

until her father wakes her to the empty room.
The men are gone. A draft of chill air lingers
in her father's hair, his rough shirt,
and together they walk the block to morning Mass.

Still dark and stars falter, then wink sharp
as shattered mirrors. Foghorns moan
and the church is cold. A few women in babushkas
kneel in the pews. Still dizzy, she follows

the priest's litanies for those who wait within
life's pale, for those departed, the shades humming
in the air, clustered thick as lake fog in the nave.
The priest elevates the wafer, a pale day moon

the spirit of God leafs through, then it's
a human face — her father's, the tired man's
and she is lost and turning through fragrant air.
Her fingers entwined make a steeple, but

all she sees is falling: the church collapsing
in shards, the great bell tolling, tolling.
1933 outside and some unwound mainspring has set
the world careening. The Jazz Age

ended years ago. Lean olive-skinned men
sport carnations and revolvers, and in the country
of her father, bankers in threadbare morning coats
wheel cartloads of currency to the bakeries

for a single loaf. The men who wait each night
outside the kitchen door have a look she's seen
in her father's eyes, although it's two years
until he turns his gentle hand against himself.

But now he touches her face. Her father stands
so straight, as if wearing a uniform he's proud of.
She watches him shape the sign of the cross.
She crosses forehead, lips, and breast, and believes,

for a moment, her father could cradle the world
in his palm. When they leave the church and its flickering
votive candles for market, it is dawn. The milkman's
wagon horse waits, patient at the curb, his breath

rosettes of steam rising to the sky that spills
like a pail of blue milk across morning. She prays
that God take care of the man in the gray coat,
that her father will live forever.

The Bookkeeper

I know the way evening shawls the mirror,
the bureau where years ago
my brother kept a lacquered box
beside the brush with its cinnabar handle.
Inside were coins, small rounds flashing
the profiles of queens and archdukes, tyrants
only history's long memory preserves.
He said we were difficult music, an endless

glissando of moods. He leaned over my shoulder
and made the shapes of notes, cupping my hands,
the keys. Tonight, the numbers are precise,
the ledger closed on the desk. I cover
the typewriter and walk home. For a moment
twilight kindles iridescent
the feathers of roosters
the Chinese grocer stacks in bamboo cages,

the strange privacy of my face through bars,
and a bird's flurry disturbing,
becoming the composition.
The first magnolias in the park
unfurl, their scent
almost an injury. Against my palm
the cane's handle curves smooth. My foot
lists in its heavy shoe.

Half a lifetime since my brother
sat with me—the operations and long shuttered
evenings with the iced drinks of summer.
He played Strauss when the gauze was removed.

He lifted me and waltzed across
the parquet, my face tucked against his neck,
the scent of bay rum. The phonograph played
into circles of static, circles of silence.

Last night I burned unanswered the letters
written on the stationery of foreign hotels.
The last from Spain, its single olive leaf
silver and bitter if held to the lips.
I imagine him ending in a port city
handling the morning papers
with gloved hands so acid won't taint
his fingers, still formal and elegant.

What could I have written? That
I don't remember his face? That I must
sit in the park with those who sit
and hear leaves blade the air, sharp,
then faltering like a flute breaking
into raggedness? That above us
the statue of a general towers? In the radiance
of streetlamps his hand extends,

as if blessing, as if conducting the orchestra
of musicians accident has assembled below him.

Night Waitress

Reflected in the plate glass, the pies
look like clouds drifting off my shoulder.
I'm telling myself my face has character,
not beauty. It's my mother's Slavic face.
She washed the floor on hands and knees
below the Black Madonna, praying
to her god of sorrows and visions
who's not here tonight when I lay out the plates,
small planets, the cups and moons of saucers.
At this hour the men all look
as if they'd never had mothers.
They do not see me. I bring the cups.
I bring the silver. There's the man
who leans over the jukebox nightly
pressing the combinations
of numbers. I would not stop him
if he touched me, but it's only songs
of risky love he leans into. The cook sings
with the jukebox, a moan and sizzle
into the grill. On his forehead
a tattooed cross furrows,
diminished when he frowns. He sings words
dragged up from the bottom of his lungs.
I want a song that rolls
through the night like a big Cadillac
past factories to the refineries
squatting on the bay, round and shiny
as the coffee urn warming my palm.
Sometimes when coffee cruises my mind
visiting the most remote way stations,
I think of my room as a calm arrival

each book and lamp in its place. The calendar
on my wall predicts no disaster
only another white square waiting
to be filled like the desire that fills
jail cells, the old arrest
that makes me stare out the window or want
to try every bar down the street.
When I walk out of here in the morning
my mouth is bitter with sleeplessness.
Men surge to the factories and I'm too tired
to look. Fingers grip lunch box handles,
belt buckles gleam, wind riffles my uniform
and it's not romantic when the sun unlids
the end of the avenue. I'm fading
in the morning's insinuations
collecting in the crevices of buildings,
in wrinkles, in every fault
of this frail machinery.

Maquillage

After nestling champagne splits in ice
I'd line the bottles behind the bar. Tapped,
they made a chilly music, *an arsenal
of bells* you called it. When I circled my arms
around myself I could count ribs
under my cotton shift. Rochelle sat at the stage's
edge warming her satin costume. She
couldn't bear the cold cloth. On the way
to your rooms I'd adjust blue lights for her.

René, that year you were the only father
I'd admit. Before opening each evening
we'd sip wine coolers on the balcony,
watch the day burn out over the square
and fountain with its cluster of stone cherubs.

With a straight razor you'd shave your face,
clean, then smooth indigo on your lids
and draw the lines of your mouth. Nights
you shook too much I'd do your face,
the wig, make you talk. It became a way
of managing the days, evening's slow descent
until the city turned in its fever
and music rose through the floor.

I'd serve while Rochelle balanced
on a sequined ball, stepping down
to the blown sound of blues. She'd gyrate
till she'd lost it all and you'd glide, joking
among tables, benevolent in a rayon kimono.

All night the river of men swerved
under their solitary stars, and we'd go on

minor players waking startled to the care
or harm of unlikely hands, surprised
to hit the lights and find the place
so shabby: numbers on the wall, the butts
and broken glass. Quiet after closing,
I'd lean by the door and smoke, hear
the fountain erode cherub faces.

You're nowhere I know anymore René.
The future we predicted is the past
and different. You're the empty room
morning pours into through a torn shade,
that place you said most nearly spells peace
in the heart, narrow glasses on the ledge
reflecting the horizon.

Tonight, children's quarreling rises
from the yard. For a moment, through shutters
the city relights itself until it's time
for music to shiver the floorboards,
the hour of plumage . . .

But that was long ago. I was only seventeen.

Jackson Hotel

Sometimes after hours of wine I can almost see
    the night gliding in low off the harbor
        down the long avenues of shop windows

past mannequins, perfect in their gestures.
    I leave water steaming on the gas ring
        and sometimes I can slip from my body,

almost find the single word to prevent evenings
    that absolve nothing, a winter lived alone
        and cold. Rooms where you somehow marry

the losses of strangers that tremble
    on the walls like the hands
        of the dancer next door, luminous

with Methedrine, she taps walls for hours
    murmuring about the silver she swears
        lines the building, the hallways

where each night drunks stammer their
    usual rosary until they come to rest
        beneath the tarnished numbers, the bulbs

that star each ceiling.
    I must tell you I am afraid to sit here
        losing myself to the hour's slow erasure

until I know myself only by this cold weight,
    this hand on my lap, palm up.
        I want to still the dancer's hands

in mine, to talk about forgiveness
   and what we leave behind—faces
      and cities, the small emergencies

of nights. I say nothing, but
   leaning on the sill, I watch her leave
      at that moment

when the first taxis start rolling
   to the lights of Chinatown, powered
      by sad and human desire. I watch her fade

down the street until she's a smudge,
   violet in the circle of my breath. A figure
      so small I could cup her in my hands.

TWO

Little Elegies

I don't know if Bonnard
would have painted the scene from my window.
Five-twenty in the morning
and the black walnut with its branch of yellow leaves
curves over the rooftops of Poole Foundry
wet from rain. In the parking lot below
a nameless agitator was shot two hours ago,
stalled for a moment beneath the blue lights
of emergency, the squad cars and pulsing sirens.

Bonnard painted wholly from memory the casual gestures
of the streets, the kitchen garden at Le Cannet
seen from the window and, with what must have been
great love, his wife Marthe. I have two prints of her
on my wall, pinned together in the way the painter worked,
two or three canvases at once.

Here he's painted a little elegy—the Midi's
transient light yellow in this print, a standing nude.
The leg of the vanity repeats in the mirror reflecting
an armoire as if the room should divide into
a series of rooms, but it's only an equation
for the atmosphere touching Marthe's back,
a lock of hair escaping her chignon. Her hand,
almost shyly, is cupped before her.

Twenty years later, Marthe is in the bath
dissolving in the wash of light on tiles
ultramarine to viridian. I can complete
what the painter leaves out: his wife crushing
lavender into water, the flowering almonds

swaying in the wind outside the house.
His way of resolving the violence of time
on his wife's body was a gentle arrest
in a churning memory of light.

He sang when he painted, eyes squinted
behind steel-framed glasses, and somehow
sitting here this fragile hour as day ignites,
it helps to watch the shadows on Marthe's ankle,
the severe yellow arch of her foot
in its violet shoe. I can almost complete

the man's face. It was mottled. On the wet pavement
rain made little shining rivers beneath his white hand,
the fingers curved almost shyly to his palm.
The sky grows lavender, the bricks sienna.
These colors, Bonnard said, *bewilder me.*

Contagion

The air swamps, static, overheated,
the kind of weather that founders a city
before a plague occurs. A fever of starlings
weights the oak's thick branches, their
nattering cries—*sex, sex*. The leaves sear
hectic as the consumptive heroine's cheeks
in the pages of the 19th-century novel
you read before the open window. She dies
so piteously; her young aristocrat bears
orchids to the antiseptic charity ward
too late to say it mattered. She coughs.
You close the book. The air stains now
with smoke, the farmers clearing stubble
from fields in this dim province of burning.

Autumn, Mist

I

This morning I took the wine from the sill
glazed perfectly in ice. It smoked down my throat,
mist across autumn fields I left in Maine
thirty years ago. I asked the mirror
if this is what it means: another room
known by heart, the Charles below
accepting everything. The city I saw on postcards
was a lie. Those shots from above, all light.

Father, my face is yours,
the way I last saw you flickering
in the doorway, tired as your eighty acres
of salt marsh and scrub pine.
Meaningless to say you were right;
the night my feet failed on the stage
of a Park Square bar, I knew it.
The men didn't look up from their drinks.

This morning tracing wrinkles from
nose to chin, I imagined them folding forever
into darkness.
Fields, dance floors—same thing—places where
soil or rhythm breaks down, where we turn
to meet ourselves.

2

It was such a simple act,
the most precise.

The fingers on the razor
might have belonged to someone else.
Over the bed, the crack in the ceiling
like the border of a country
I could never quite recall. Water rushes
in pipes, the drain needs fixing.
In the dark, it doesn't matter.
My dancing shoes, worn down at the heels
lean against each other in the closet.

Jacques will creep
up the stairs, shoes in hand, tired
from waiting tables. He steps so lightly
as if his late return is a matter of concern.
He should always be serving, always be leaning
over candles, eyes mauved in strained circles.

He'll bring rolls in white paper
as always. Tomorrow, he'll unpin the print
from the wall, Picasso — a woman ironing,
everything falling in blue gravity,
so tired, as if she desires only to sink
from the weight of her body.

       3

And, perhaps, the body
really is a gift, this small beating
in my ribs a reasoned rhythm. Once, a woman
at the museum reminded me of a harp. Her supple spine
defined a frame. She was so tense, I could see wires

as if at any moment she would become music
or break. The way moonlight broke itself
in our window when as children
we sisters cut each other's hair.
Mary and I found a moth trapped in butter —
wings
a purple diagram of stopped motion.

At Thirty

Whole years I knew only nights: automats
& damp streets, the Lower East Side steep

with narrow rooms where sleepers turn beneath
alien skies. I ran when doorways spoke

rife with smoke & zippers. But it was only the heart's
racketing flywheel stuttering *I want, I want*

until exhaustion, until I was a guest in the yoke
of my body by the last margin of land where the river

mingles with the sea & far off daylight whitens,
a rending & yielding I must kneel before, as

barges loose glittering mineral freight
& behind me façades gleam with pigeons

folding iridescent wings. Their voices echo
in my voice naming what is lost, what remains.

Diamonds

Only once had I seen the diamonds worn:
at the funeral of the scarlet parrot, my sister
draped herself in velvet, musty from the attic
trunk, then chanted over the shoebox we buried
with a watch and three Russian coins. On her hands
the rings sparkled a trance over geraniums
banked on the grave. I know I looked foolish,
a boy in black tights kneeling to smooth the earth.
I believed the soul was fire, and waited
that night for the bird to soar in flames
over the sleeping house, beyond Grandmother's
room thick with her odors of menthol and garlic.
We had only each other, Manya and I
and Grandmother, her long dying,
with that ivory backscratcher shaped like a claw
on her table. In her illness, she wished herself
back sometimes to the flat on Railroad Street,
or sealed again in the casket, smuggled
from her village to the sea, those rings pinned
in her blouse. There was no ease in this remembering.
She'd startle and cry out in the old language.
I carried the soup, the glass syringe, and I
wished her dead when I stood by the window, silent.
When she called *Petrushka, Petrushka*, I hid in drapes
that closed around me, many whispering hands.
Manya rubbed her legs with black salve, and when
Grandmother died, I did not watch for a wreath
of fire. We found rubles and war bonds
sewn in the mattress, and months after we discovered
useless currency stitched in dresses, folded
in books she could not read.

For fifteen years her room has been empty—the house
Manya's now. She does not like me to come there.
Still, it had been easy to slip the diamonds
from the trunk, to walk all night the streets
of narrow houses with my coat drawn close against
the first chills, the cramping muscles. Trees
rustle in my ears, pages from some vast police
report, loosing leaves over the avenues
and freight yards lit with ashcan fires.
Sometimes I long to be smoke, rising up, away
from the body's shrill needs, those acts and hours
gone wrong. After I touched her, I'd wash my hands
over and over. Last week I remembered this
by the window of my room. There was a moon like
an oily bubble in the sky and my hands on the sill
were those of a foreigner, each vein a river,
scarred. And who, this morning
among these faces filing to work, these clerks
and secretaries, would crave this embrace?
Yet aren't they all speechlessly in love
with bad news, some private disgrace sheltered
in a doorway among those spread out before me?

At the street of gin mills and penny-ante
arcades, I pause and smooth my sleeves.
The pawn sign is tarnished, the taste of myself
as I stand before the broker. On the wall
a photo of Sonny Liston shadowboxes a postcard—
Pope John gazing, serenely, above the broker's
lacquered pompadour. He watches me unravel
the handkerchief, then squinting through

his jeweler's glass, he slides the rings across
his velvet tray. Wings burn behind my eyes
when he calls the diamonds poor, as I nod
to a price too low. *All she'd wanted*
were her saints, a little morphine. The shop fan
inflicts its breeze over my face, and seized
by the trembling, I turn toward the street
where shadows pool like black waters, toward
the traffic's effortless passage. I'd risen
once from the waters of sleep
to my grandmother's face framed by the smoke
of her hair. In the nightlight, she stood
over me, as now, like an angel of reckoning
swayed by a powerful and secret weeping.

A System

All week, floods throughout the South.
Beneath a beer sign's floating rings
I wait for the rain to clear in this bar
where the patrons are mostly the blind
from the state school down the street.
They gaze at the TV's flawed picture: wrestlers
limned in blue light, the feminine soothing
of the trainer's hands. Beside me
at her table, Nina strokes her dog
to calmness, tilts her third bourbon.
Once, she told me how her mother
had kept hidden for decades
the Lithuanian coins that blistered
her brother's eyes—dead at four of measles.
Across the scarred table her hands
flutter, moth wings, a touch soft
as my great-aunt's years ago
tracing my forehead, my lips.
She had cataracts, the eye's filming, milky
and named for falling water. In her sunporch
she read to me of rivers and palaces until I saw
the pages were all wrong, the words
mere remembered cadences. At dusk
when lamps came on they stood,
she said, haloed like angels.
She crossed her hands over my eyes
and closed me into the mind's
green pacific room. That night I prayed
for her, a child's bargaining with God.
Tonight, in a blue half-light
of faces, blindness seems immense

as the lucid hours of insomnia—
somewhere a scarf's shadow grows
dangerous over the clock's face
glowing with the numerals
of 3:16 a.m. In my hand
the glass is chilled and prayer
is simply waiting for the mind to float
into precision, to still. Soon
I'll drive home through flooded streets.
Nina in her room will change her wet dress
for a gown discovered slowly
by a system of tags and textures. I want her
then, to sit quietly, in a pure matrix
of imagined light, darkness pressing down
like rain as the radio plays stations
from Baton Rouge, New Orleans, and beyond.

Preparing the Estate Sale

This woman, this Marie Brousseau,
saved everything, a recluse receiving
foodstamp groceries, the medicines of old age.
I must soak her figurines in water
that darkens as dust floats from their skirts.
Air will dry them, high summer and magnolias choking
the house. Crystal wine stems glitter
on shelves among dolls turned
so their porcelain faces view the walls,
washed now where Marie scrawled private arguments
in China marker—opening in English, ending
in the imperfect time of French verbs.
But this damp. This kitchen. This plaster.

How do I assess the last twenty years:
the way she tested her eyesight daily with charts,
the large E faltering over the stove, the vanity
and this accretion of dresses?
Generations of her hats litter
the divan behind me, afternoon diminishing
as I mark buttonhooks and beaded purses in this shocked air
there's nothing delicate about, these paper sacks
on shelves in every room—vials of tannic acid,
charcoal and milk of magnesium, her Universal Poison Antidote.

Polishing the legs of chairs, the only toxin
is time—my face in the mirror,
clocks throughout the house arranged
by a private chronology, as if she could reverse
the way our lives pass so gracelessly from our hands.

She's younger in these photos than I am:
1925, Marie disembarks from France, New Orleans,
her face under a cloche, eyes vague smudges.
The dock must have smelled of oysters and chicory.
Or here, she reclines in a wicker chaise,
one of those green and cream evenings
the South is famous for, deep June.
She looks frankly at the camera, as if the future
would be kind, as if her life
could never drift unmoored.

Marie, I'm talking to you now. I'm asking you
who will smooth the wrinkles from my dresses?
Will it be someone so unknown
as to be past imagining? Someone discarding
my husband's letters, these notes to myself falling
contagious as leaves in this green hushed light
that indicts everything.
May they not judge us severely.

THREE

Chinese New Year

The dragon is in the street dancing beneath windows
    pasted with colored squares, past the man
who leans into the phone booth's red pagoda, past
    crates of doves and roosters veiled

until dawn. Fireworks complicate the streets
    with sulphur as people exchange gold
and silver foil, money to appease ghosts
    who linger, needy even in death. I am

almost invisible. Hands could pass through me
    effortlessly. This is how it is
to be so alien that my name falls from me, grows
    untranslatable as the shop signs,

the odors of ginseng and black fungus that idle
    in the stairwell, the corridor where
the doors are blue mouths ajar. Hands
    gesture in the smoke, the partial moon

of a face. For hours the soft numeric
    click of mah-jongg tiles drifts
down the hallway where languid Mai trails
    her musk of sex and narcotics.

There is no grief in this, only the old year
    consuming itself, the door knob blazing
in my hand beneath the lightbulb's electric jewel.
    Between voices and fireworks

wind works bricks to dust—*hush, hush*—
    no language I want to learn. I can touch
the sill worn by hands I'll never know
    in this room with its low table

where I brew chrysanthemum tea. The sign
    for Jade Palace sheds green corollas
on the floor. It's dangerous to stand here
    in the chastening glow, darkening

my eyes in the mirror with the gulf of the rest
    of my life widening away from me, waiting
for the man I married to pass beneath
    the sign of the building, to climb

the five flights and say his Chinese name for me.
    He'll rise up out of the puzzling streets
where men pass bottles of rice liquor, where
    the new year is liquor, the black bottle

the whole district is waiting for, like
    some benevolent arrest—the moment
when men and women turn to each other and dissolve
    each bad bet, every sly mischance,

the dalliance of hands. They turn in lamplight
    the way I turn now. Wai Min is in the doorway.
He brings fish. He brings lotus root.
    He brings me ghost money.

Arias, 1971

It was her hair I always noticed, rippling
as she walked the hallway to our flat
below the opera singer who'd rehearse
until evening, her arias. China Doll battled
sometimes with her AWOL junkie lover—curses

and plates shattering the wall. Her son
sputtered airplane sounds and beat the radiator
with a spoon, wise already to what smolders
out of helplessness. I closed my door.
When autumn turned bitter, we taped newspaper

over the panes and those winter nights
we rode the subway from Symphony to Chinatown
where I poured drinks at the Phoenix
and she hustled bars, the gambling houses.
The train rocked and windows gave our faces back

ghost twins, sisters from some other life.
China brushed her hair, coal black, until
it sparked, and if I closed my eyes the rails sang
raven wing, forbidden heart, bright cinder.
One long dusk I sat as her child

practiced his numbers, 5's and the 8's
he'd scrawl like those botched infinities
I'd drawn in high school notebooks
below the signs for man and woman, the sign
for death. China leaned over her spoon,

the match's wavering blue tongue,
over the shadow and soft skin of her arm.
Nothing to lose, she laughed,
nothing. Her strap slid from her shoulder
to show the crescent scar above her breast.

She slow-danced with herself across the room,
vagrant hair swaying. Swaying, her face tilted
heavenward and the low pulse in her throat.
Upstairs the opera singer began again
Desdemona's final prayers for mercy

from a silent God. The aria soared and fell
and carried us out to December streets
milling with late shoppers, their breath chilled,
perishable, the season a paradise of dolls
and trains, the steaming subway vents.

That last time I saw her, we walked the blocks
to Washington, paused at a shop window: a pyramid
of televisions all tuned to Walter Cronkite.
His mouth shaped silent phrases. And then it began —
the roll call of war dead. Their names sailing

upward, ash, and we had everything
to lose. Snowing, and the wind lashed
China's hair, a hand
across her face, mine.
I tell you, it was snowing.

Hollywood Jazz

Who says it's cool says wrong.
　For it rises from the city's
　　　sweltering geometry of rooms,

fire escapes, and flares from the heels
　of corner boys on Occidental
　　　posing with small-time criminal

intent—all pneumatic grace. This
　is the music that plays at the moment
　　　in every late-night *noir* flick

when the woman finds herself alone, perfectly
　alone, in a hotel room before a man
　　　whose face is so shadowed as to be

invisible, one more bedroom arsonist
　seeing nothing remotely
　　　cool: a woman in a cage

of half-light, Venetian blinds.
　This is where jazz blooms, in the hook
　　　and snag of her zipper opening to

an enfilade of trumpets. Her dress
　falls in a dizzy indigo riff.
　　　I know her vices are minor: sex,

forgetfulness, the desire to be someone,
　anyone else. On the landing, the man
　　　pauses before descending

one more flight. Checks his belt. Adjusts
    the snap brim over his face. She smoothes
        her platinum hair and smokes a Lucky

to kill his cologne. And standing there
    by the window in her slip, midnight blue,
        the stockings she did not take off,

she is candescent, her desolation
    a music so voluptuous I want
        to linger with her. And if I do not

turn away from modesty or shame,
    I'm in this for keeps, flying with her
        into fear's random pivot where each article

glistens like evidence: the tube of lipstick,
    her discarded earrings. When she closes
        her eyes, she hears the streetcar's

nocturne up Jackson, a humpbacked sedan
    rounding the corner from now
        to that lavish void of tomorrow,

a sequence of rooms: steam heat, modern,
    2 bucks. Now listen. Marimbas.
        His cologne persists, a redolence

of fire alarms, and Darling,
    there are no innocents here, only
        dupes, voyeurs. On the stairs

he flicks dust from his alligator
    shoes. I stoop to straighten
        the seams of my stockings, and

when I meet him in the shadows
    of the stairwell, clarinets whisper
        Here, take my arm. Walk with me.

The Charmed Hour

for my mother

On the radio, gypsy jazz. Django Reinhardt
   puts a slow fire to Ellington's *Solitude*
      while ice cubes pop in your martini. The sting
of lime on my palm. By the sink you lean,
   twisting your rings. Turn to the window.

In shadow you could be sixteen
   again, in your mother's kitchen
      above Cleveland, the cafés of Warsaw still
smoky in your mind with talk and cigarettes,
   English still a raw mystery of verbs.

Windows brighten across the city at the hour
   when voices steam from the street
      like some sadness—the charmed hour
when, smooth as brilliantine, Phil Verona
   with his Magic Violin slides from the radio.

Ice-blue in silk, his All-Girl Orchestra sways
   through the parlor. You let yourself
      step with them, let a gardenia release
its vanilla scent in your hair.
   Over terraces, you dance above vapor-lights,

Gold Coast streets where club doors swing
   like the doors of banks that never fail.
      In back rooms men and women spend themselves
over green baize tables, the ivory poker chips.
   In their chests wings beat, steady

as the longing wakened to from every dream
   of flying. We could shut the door
      on this vertigo, but Mother when we
come to ourselves our feet skim the tiles.
   Spoons shine on the table, and Mother,

we're dancing. I'm mouthing the words
   to a song I never knew, singing when
      evening arrives and flattens the sky
to a last yellow crease of light,
   thin as a knife, as a wish.

The Floating Wedding

Awake she's wedded to the stranger
in herself, her hands in climateless light,

nails smooth and blue. Nothing has changed.
Her husband sleeps. The cabin fills

with slight bitterness, carnations
returning their small fires to air.

Nothing has changed. The wedding over,
guests ferried back to the pier, only

artifacts of marriage remain, heavy knives,
the wedding cake sodden and littered

with the confetti of good cheer.
She watches on shore a single headlamp.

It's the drunk. She knows him, has seen him
in the streets of the village, knows

he's been asked to leave the homosexual bars,
the slim forbidden boys with faces dark

and watery as those in aquatints. Nightly
he struggles with the bicycle through sand

past floating piers and houses with their freight
of sleep. She'd like to spare the old man

his blind driving into night
a little while. She'd like to sit and drink,

maybe talk or ease his trembling,
incurable as the singleness returned to

after passion. Turning away
she lowers her veil to the sea,

its crown of flowers floating
like a doll's small funeral barge.

When she wraps her arms around herself
she is wrapped in a blue fire. She touches

her husband's whitening shoulder. She'll sleep
and not witness the way the old man

suffers dawn, not witness
the night moving off over the sea,

drifting with its burden of longing
to darken the other half of the world.

Remington

It's hot—the evening could so easily erupt
to a fusillade of sirens. Then I'd take the arm
of a passing stranger, whirl him startled
in a brisk flamenco. There'd be a knife,
some roses. But these are the vapors of summer.

I sit on the railing, smoke, and watch
the teenage mothers of Remington stroll
their babies, shaking back their razor-cut hair
to the wail of blues rolling through the screens
of narrow apartments. Evenly, the words wash

the faces of men on stoops in stained workshirts,
half-moons of grease under their nails, the faces
of the unemployed who have all day taken refuge
from the blinding streets in the museums
of pool halls and taverns, over the women

fanning themselves, crescents of sweat spoiling
their sleeveless dresses. There's nothing to do
about it, but see the shapes the music makes
of us, as if we were moved by some larger volition:
across the street, A-Jay's out of jail delivered

by the seamless hands of the Public Defender.
The neighbor woman told me how, wild one night
last week, he shot out each mirror in the house,
then stayed locked inside for hours. She waved
the air between us, clucked softly to herself.

Quiet tonight, he sits in the doorway,
loose change in his pockets and the Pimlico sheet
inked with the numbers and handicaps of each stable.
Each horse scrawled on a paper scrap, arranged,
rearranged. Around a cigarette, he mutters

the sweet inflammatory names: Mere Scintilla,
Lark's Dream, Fair Charleen, and everything
they spell of the miraculous legs that bear
such violent hopes. Chestnuts and bays
sport jockey's bright silks, glories fleeting

as the current of wind that lifts and eddies
his paper scraps. Lately,
these details are precious to me:
a cigarette's fiery arc, the brief filigree
of shadow across a stranger's shoulders

as night falls and catches the voice
of Jay's woman. Framed in the doorway,
she bends, gathers the scattered notations.
She tells her friend, *When he gets this way,*
he just tears my clothes off. Just tears them off.

Housekeeping Cottages

A tin flamingo rhumbas with a mermaid,
their thin music spins through the window
to Harry tipped back in his deck chair,
his cigarette making smoke patches over
the Monopoly board. When he squints, the smoke blends
with the breaker's foam. His kids scream
at the tideline, their beach ball bobbing
in surf, mild and green.

Dot brings back two cold ones he opens
with a church key. Each summer they leave
Jersey's industrial stacks,
the sun blazing off the sides
of aluminum diners. Harry likes the rows
of saltboxes shuttered clean
in blue, the long terra-cotta walkway that banks
and curves into the seawall. He likes the riffle
of play money, the way the game lasts
all vacation. It's Dot's turn

and she shakes the dice a long time.
He likes the sound and the sense of his life
edging the sea. She throws and Harry watches
her thigh tense, her legs big,
absolutely smooth. When she leans to read
the dice, Jungle Gardenia wafts across
the table. Her flatiron scrapes to Marvin Gardens
and the kids are screaming, running
after the shadow of a blimp, their mouths
small black circles.

In his palm the racecar token warms
as he waits for Dot to oil her shoulders.
He doesn't mind waiting. He can do it for hours
like sometimes at night smoking
hearing the sea's invisible drag. That's when
he thinks about the Olds, robin's-egg blue,
he longs for. The wheels would shine
and ride him smoothly down the avenues,
a little dangerous, passing hotels and women
in doorways with permed blond haloes.

He drops his cigarette into an empty.
It sizzles as he lights another, then rolls.
A double, two sixes. He roars his car
down Boardwalk, its diamonds and expensive faces.
Past GO, hit the bank and cruise the purple
side streets, Mediterranean and Baltic. At Chance
Harry draws a card. Harry goes to jail
and does not collect. In the sky
the blimp looks like a slim cigar
its wrapper unfurling behind it, a banner
Harry can't make out.

Spring

If only we'd arrived without history
at this room thick with columns
of steam. No stairways leading
up or down, only this room given to sky,

eclipsing the garden, the bottling plant,
and mill houses. Then all I'd need
to know would be here among towels,
the porcelain tub and shock of forsythia

slipping my fingers down each vertebra
of the spine's perishable harp. These shy
wings—your shoulders which have stooped
all day over sorrowing accounts.

Light pierces the pane, glazes water
spilling from my hands over your hair.
This thin vein across your temple.
The factory whistle shrills and men walk

from locked trunks to their cars
at that time once called *the gloaming*
when the sky holds a dense glow
and voices shimmer then drift like shadows

netted among the branches of mulberry
and linden below the porch where we linger
over shrimp, Greek cheese. It's April,
the evening's cool and far off

the neon advertisements speak
only to themselves. They remind you
of the tangled circuits of your father's mind,
injured months ago — a drunken accident

on winter roads. Sometimes he mistakes you
for his brother or a younger self,
his workman's hands dangling, tapered
long like yours, but awkward

in the hospital gown's loose folds.
Because sleep is difficult he watches
all night the hills of the city hammered
with light, the half-moon blazing

steep streets, mazes of alleys
and cul de sacs that carried us to this turning,
calmly entering each other's histories.
Difficult son of that father, I'll hold you

until we arrive at a radical simplicity:
this room suspended over trees enlarging
in the deep vault of spring,
your damp hair cool against my cheek.

Invisible Gestures

The way geodes can be cracked to reveal ears
perfectly listening to crystal, you could crack
open this picture and find anything.
A man, a woman in scarves
at a table
that like the sea and sky behind them
might, at any moment,
vaporize into blue. Netted
with invisible gestures
sky and sea persist
the only certainty in our traveling.

For it's possible she has been traveling
all night. A train
with frame after frame
unraveling behind her. Pastures where cows continue
in the dark, unseen. Station lights
pin faces into the ivory of untroubled repose,
the repose of long waiting
for a scheduled event. Perhaps
she is traveling to leave her face behind,
an unremarkable woman closer to *thirty-five*
than herself. She notices telephone wires
link the country with the urgency
and tenuousness of a late-night call.

It is possible the man has been sleepless,
waiting. Maybe failing to reconstruct
the floor plans of every place
he has ever lived, he strikes a match.
In the flame his palm curls toward him,

shell-pink as a waiting ear,
and for the first time, down streets,
he hears the chain of desire and expectation
that moves the world. His cigarette smoke
will stop at the ceiling
as in the frame of this moment
every street, every track narrows
into a point of blue.

As the shadows and halftones of their nights
contain the day's salvation,
it's possible they believe,
even at this late date,
beyond the surface
a man and a woman shelter a miracle,
the salt of their hands.

Accretion

Consider autumn,
   its violent candling
      of hours: birches

& beach plums flare harsh,
   chrome-yellow, orange,
      the dog zigzags the hillside

tangled with flaming vines
   to the pond below & barks
      at the crows' reflected flight,

a reverse swimming
   among water lilies, that
      most ancient of flowers

anchored by muscular stems
   in the silt of cries
      & roots, tenacious as the mind's

common bloom, remembered men
   I have touched at night
      in the room

below the African painter's
   empty loft, his few abandoned
      canvases, narratives

of drought & famine, of how
   his people, hands linked
      entered the deepest cave,

the unbearable heart
  of belief where each gesture
    encloses the next — clouds

packed densely as ferns, becoming
  coal, the final diamond
    of light, the god's return

as rain, its soft insistence
  loosening the yellowed hands
    of leaves that settle

at my feet. How expendable
  & necessary this mist
    in my hair, these jewels

beading the dog's wet coat.
  How small I am
    beneath this vast sway.

Star Ledger

In memory of Mary Green Hull

How perilous to choose not
to love the life we're shown.
> *Seamus Heaney*

ONE

Star Ledger

Almost time to dress for the sun's total eclipse
   so the child pastes one last face
in her album of movie stars — Myrna Loy
   and Olivia de Havilland — names meant to conjure
sultry nights, voluptuous turns across
   some dance floor borne on clouds. Jean Harlow.

Clipped from the Newark evening paper, whole galaxies
   of splendid starlets gaze, fixed to violet pages
spread drying on the kitchen table. The child whispers
   their names when she tests "lorgnettes"
made that morning out of shirtboards, old film
   negatives gleaned from her grandmother's hat box.

Through phony opera glasses, hall lights blur
   stained sepia above her, and her grandmother's
room is stained by a tall oak's crown, yellow
   in the window. Acorns crack against asphalt
three floors down. The paper promised
   "a rare conjunction of sun and moon and earth."

Her grandmother brushed thick gray hair.
   Cut glass bottles and jewel cases.
Above the corset her back was soft, black moles
   she called her "melanomas" dusted across
powdery skin like a night sky, inside out.
   The Spanish fan dangles from her wrist

and when she stands she looks like an actress
   from the late-night movies. The child sifts
costume brooches, glass rubies and sapphires,

to find the dark gold snake ring with emerald chips
for eyes. She carries the miniature hourglass
    to the sagging porch, then waiting turns it over

and over. Uncertain in high heels, she teeters
    and the shawl draped flamenco-style keeps sliding off
her shoulder, so she glances up the block to Girl Scouts
    reeling down the flag. The child hates their dull uniforms,
how they scatter shrieking through leafsmoke and the sheen
    of fallen chestnuts. She touches the ring, heavy

on a ribbon circling her neck, then thinks she'll sew
    the album pages with green embroidery silk.
Her grandmother snaps the fan and they raise lorgnettes
    to the sun's charcoaled face, its thin wreath
of fire. Quiet, the Girl Scouts bow their heads—sleek
    Italian ones and black girls with myriad tight braids.

Streetlights hum on, then the towers of Manhattan flare
    beyond the river. The earth must carve its grave ellipse
through desert space, through years and histories
    before it will cross with sun and moon this way again.
Minor starlets in the child's album will fade and tatter,
    fleeting constellations with names flimsy as

the shawl that wraps her shoulders. She'll remember
    this as foolish. The girls by the flag will mostly leave
for lives of poverty, crippled dreams, and Newark
    will collapse to burn like another dying star.

But none of this has happened. Afternoon has stilled
  with the eclipse that strips them of their shadows,

so each one stands within their own brief human orbit
  while the world reverses, then slowly, recovers.

Shore Leave

She wears the sailor suit—a blouse with anchors,
skirt puffed in stiff tiers above her thin
knees, those spit-shined party shoes. Behind her
a Cadillac's fabulous fins gleam and reflected
in the showroom window, her father's a mirage.
The camera blocks his face as he frames
a shot that freezes her serious grin,
the splendid awkwardness of almost-adolescence.
He's all charm with the car dealer and fast-talks
them a test-drive in a convertible like the one
on display, a two-tone Coupe de Ville. But once
around the corner he lowers the top and soon
they're fishtailing down dump-truck paths,
the Jersey Meadows smoldering with trash fires.
He's shouting *Maybelline, why can't you be true,*
and seagulls lift in a tattered curtain across
Manhattan's hazy skyline. Dust-yellow clouds
behind him, he's handsome as a matinée idol,
wavy hair blown straight by sheer velocity.
Tall marsh weeds bend, radiant as her heart's
relentless tide. They rip past gaping Frigidaires,
rusted hulks of cranes abandoned to the weather.
Her father teases her she's getting so pretty
he'll have to jump ship sometime and take her
on a real whirl, maybe paint the whole town red.
For her *merchant marine* conjures names like
condiments—Malabar, Marseilles—places where
the laws of gravity don't hold. She can't believe
her father's breakneck luck will ever run out.
He accelerates and spins out as if the next thrill
will break through to some more durable joy.

So she stands, hands atop the windshield and shouts
the chorus with him, and later when they drop the car
he takes her to a cocktail bar and plays Chuck Berry
on the jukebox. She perches on a barstool and twirls
her Shirley Temple's paper umbrella, watches
the slick vinyl disks stack up, rhythms collecting,
breaking like surf as her father asks the barmaid
to dance with him through "Blue Moon," then foamy
glass after glass of beer. The barmaid's sinuous
in red taffeta, a rhinestone choker around
her throat. Her father's forgotten her and dances
a slow, slow tango in the empty bar and the dark
comes on like the tiny black rose on the barmaid's
shoulder rippling under her father's hand.
The girl thinks someday she'll cover her skin
with roses, then spins, dizzy on the barstool.
She doesn't hear the woman call her foolish
mortal father a two-bit trick because she's whirling
until the room's a band of light continuous
with the light the city's glittering showrooms throw
all night long over the sleek, impossible cars.

Fairy Tales: Steel Engravings

Dusk after dusk, through the smoke of industry
and autumn buffed across the sky, the shy girl
loses herself in books her grandmother once read
as a child. Blue and violet spines shine

in her hands, gilt-edged pages and those stories
of runaway children transformed to sea urchins
caught by underwater journeys. At some point
in her mind, the Thames and Hudson braid their waters

and below, the traffic flows like the river flows
across the pages, steely, engraved with whorls
and the salesgirls wave from curbs and bus-stop
islands like good children left behind, sketched

on riverbanks or sleeping the sleep
of a different century. The playground cries
of Catholic girls across the street filter
through the curtains to her reading chair

and although they surely know the soul
is a white, clear room they carry with them, they
seem so purely physical, unbound in blue gym suits,
cool air stippling their skin. Nuns' faces

from sidelines float, bodiless, the girl believes,
on columns of air, their habits shirring the wind.
The girl looks back to her book and her grandmother's
humming through a clatter of enamelware and radio news

from Cuba, then the Aqueduct race results—
Fred Caposella chanting a spell of Caribbean jockeys'
names steaming through the alarm of garlic
and rosemary that clouds the panes of London

where yellow squares of gaslight show the way
home to solitary walkers draped in bracelets,
thin collars of fog. Beyond the parlor windows
the girl sees women turn in heavy silks through

brittle rings of gossip that rise up the stairwell
to the empty nursery, an open window where
their children have descended ladders of white mist,
and it's too late to call them home from the river's

quick current. Already the bridges have closed
over them, arms embracing, letting go
those children whose bodies swiftly grow
strange, paradisal. Book open on her lap, the girl's

already in love with promises of transport. She traces
the caps of engraved sea-leaves that frame those faces
like sunflowers turning to follow the moon's silver
imperative that lays a ruler across the waves, the tides

where her story begins in the surge and lapse of traffic.
She hears *Bay of Pigs* then *Odds 10 to 1,* and the cries
fading, now turning sharper across the street as if
by sheer volume, each girl might stay her departure.

Love Song during Riot with Many Voices

Newark, 1967

The bridge's iron mesh chases pockets of shadow
and pale through blinds shuttering the corner window

to mark this man, this woman, the young eclipse
their naked bodies make—black, white, white,
black, the dying fall of light rendering bare walls

incarnadine, color of flesh and blood occluded

in voices rippling from the radio: Saigon besieged,
Hanoi, snipers and the riot news helicoptered
from blocks away. All long muscle, soft

hollow, crook of elbow bent sequined above the crowd,
nightclub dancers farandole their grind and slam
into streets among the looters. Let's forget the 58¢

lining his pockets, forget the sharks and junkyards

within us. Traffic stalls to bricks shattering,
the windows, inside her, bitch I love you, city breaking
down and pawnshops disgorge their contraband of saxophones

and wedding rings. Give me a wig, give me
a pistol. Hush baby, come to papa, let me hold you

through night's broken circuitry, chromatic
and strafed blue with current. Let's forget this bolt
of velvet fallen from a child's arm brocading

pavement where rioters careen in furs and feathered hats
burdened with fans, the Polish butcher's strings

of sausages, fat hams. This isn't a lullaby a parent
might croon to children before sleep, but all of it
belongs: in the station torn advertisements whisper
easy credit, old men wait for any train out of town

and these lovers mingling, commingling their bodies,
this slippage, a haul and wail of freight trains

pulling away from the yards. With this girl
I'll recall black boys by the soda shop, other times
with conked pompadours and scalloped afterburns
stenciled across fenders. Through the radio

Hendrix butanes his guitar to varnish, crackle
and discord of "Wild Thing." Sizzling strings,
that Caravaggio face bent to ask the crowd

did they want to see him sacrifice something
he loved. Thigh, mouth, breast, small of back, dear
hollow of the throat, don't you understand this pressure,

of hotbox apartments? There's no forgetting the riot
within, fingernails sparking to districts
rivering with flame. What else could we do

but cling and whisper together as children after
the lullaby is done, but no, never as children, never

do they so implore, oh god, god, bend your dark visage

over this acetylene skyline, over Club Zanzibar
and the Best of Three, limed statues in the parks, over
the black schoolgirl whose face is smashed again

and again. No journalist for these aisles of light
the cathedral spots cast through teargas and the mingling,
commingling of sisters' voices in chapels, storefront
churches asking for mercy.

                Beyond the bridge's
iron mesh, the girl touches a birthmark
behind her knee and wishes the doused smell
of charred buildings was only hydrants flushing hot concrete.

Summertime. Pockets of shadow and pale. Too hot
to sleep, Hush baby, come to papa, board
the window before morning's fractured descant,

a staccato crack of fire escapes snapping pavement
and citizens descending, turning back with points of flame

within their eyes before they too must look away.
At dawn, when the first buses leave, their great wipers arc
like women bending through smoke

to burdens, singing terror, singing pity.

Midnight Reports

That's how billboards give up their promises—
they look right into your window, then whisper
sex, success. The Salem girl's smoke plume
marries the gulf between the high-rise projects,
the usual knife's edge ballet enacted nightly there
for the benefit of no one. It's just that
around midnight every love I've known flicks open
like a switchblade and I have to start talking,
talking to drown out the man in the radio
who instructs me I'm on the edge of a new day
in this city of Newark which is not a city

of roses, just one big hockshop. I can't tell you
how it labors with its grilled storefronts, air
rushing over the facts of diamonds, appliances,
the trick carnations. But you already know that.
The M-16 Vinnie sent—piece by piece—from Vietnam
is right where you left it the day you skipped town
with the usherette of the Paradise Triple-X Theater.
You liked the way she played her flashlight down
those rows of men, plaster angels flanked around
that screen. Sometimes you'd go fire rounds over
the landfill, said it felt better than crystal meth,
a hit that leaves a trail of neon, ether.

I keep it clean, oiled, and some nights it seems
like a good idea to simply pick up that rifle
and hold it, because nothing's safe. You know
how it is: one minute you're dancing, the next you're flying
through plate glass and the whole damn town is burning
again with riots and looters, the bogus politicians.

We'd graduated that year, called the city ours,
a real bed of Garden State roses. I've drawn x's
over our eyes in the snapshot Vinnie took commencement
night, a line of x's over our linked hands. The quartet
onstage behind us sang a cappella — four brothers
from Springfield Ave. spinning in sequined tuxedos,

palms outstretched to the crowd, the Latin girls
from Ironbound shimmering in the brief conflagration
of their beauty, before the kids, before
the welfare motels, corridors of cries and exhalations.
I wore the heels you called my blue suede shoes,
and you'd given yourself a new tattoo, my name across
your bicep, in honor of finishing, in honor of the future
we were arrogant enough to think would turn out right.
I was laughing in that picture, laughing when the rain
caught us later and washed the blue dye from my shoes —
blue, the color of bruises, of minor regrets.

The Real Movie, with Stars

The tide foams in with its cargo of debris, and this man,
delirious in evening clothes, kneels begging me *please*

and it doesn't matter who I am or that he's never
seen me. Off-season, the boardwalk's empty pay phone rings

through the chemical Atlantic's curse and slap.
What can I say? Me, another stranger with empty pockets,

bad habits, unpacking my sequence of crises vanquished, surpassed
then spread upon the beach between us. He's staggered away

and it's as if I'm swimming in a theater's musk of plush,
watching myself drunk again on blanched sunlight, the lethal

hum of oleander, whatever ravening thing we want that's
so illusory. Los Angeles. The audience shuffles

while in the balcony a man weeps before the film commences.
That concrete arroyo I, someone not I, wandered once

through blurred frames to this two-bit Sonoran rodeo—everyone
swilling beer around a chestnut gelding, shoulders lathered,

his nostrils tortured to a rude facsimile of roses. Such breath,
such confounding brilliance, this slim Mexican saying *estrella*,

estrellita, fingering my blond hair. Maybe it was the sunglasses.
Or a tincture of sweat and panic like that streaking

the forehead of the B-movie actress playing someone's
discarded mistress down on a binge, reeling stupidly through

pastel hallucinated alleys seeking amnesia's salt tequila sting.
A stranger with formal collar and cummerbund. Someplace

where there are no casual encounters. But tonight, a continent away
there's the salt kiss, full on the mouth, of another ceaseless ocean

bestowing gnarled rafts of weed, the styrofoam and high heels.
I wasn't supposed to be in that arroyo. The Mexicans

weren't supposed to be in the country. Larger and larger
circles of not belonging, as if we belonged anywhere

marooned in our tidepools of tiaras and razors, little kits
brought along for the ride. As if anything, finally, belongs to us—

those intangible empires of fear and regret, sudden
crests of tenderness. Even the soul, some would hold,

escapes to a vast celestial band wrapping the world
without us. In Los Angeles, a beige froth of haze

hid the mountains. *Estrellita*, and what gone thing
did the Mexican recall in that turning? A girl's dusky hand

cradling fruit with silvery skin, coiled pulp the tint of roses
in mist? Or was it dust cascading from the tipped palm, La Pelona,

that old bald uncle, Death, spitting on a barroom floor?
In this movie time's running out. The Mexican touched my hair

and I took the kiss full on the mouth, sweet fruit, miraculous
chemistry of salts and water that keeps the flesh, that swells

and spills and feels so like weeping. What belongs to me,
if not this? Given splendor by the pay phone's luminescence,

the man wearing evening clothes slumps upon the boardwalk.
Perhaps he is the messenger beneath these chilling stars,

these heavenly infernos, burning here above the sea.

So Many Swimmers

Confettied to shreds, the last leaves darken
      gusts that shrug passersby
into winter. On the sill, a fly's husk rattles
      its hollow cartouche, photos

spread across the table in this perishing slant
      of afternoon. Distant
with afterlife's opacity, my friend's face shadows
      the surface, so many cherished

strangers, the stolen kiss returned with its burden.
      Again, the struck chord
of some rapt entropic melody, the static fall
      of a kimono from alabaster

shoulders. Was it a blue room or a shade more sheer
      like gauze fluting the brow?
Was the white piano by the wall, crumbling plaster
      and ivy twining to espalier

the inside of this place, the mind's edge glimpsed
      by half-sleep? Calm is
apparitional at times like these, December's first
      gale from the sea rocking

this ship of a house in surge and creak, water
      foaming the road. Before me,
the photos fan the hour's edge, my friend caught
      like this—angle of bone,

aquiline bridge too visible through translucent skin.
        Savage out there.
Fence pickets undo themselves from next-door's yard
        where a television fills

with snow. Capricious nature, this uneasy providence,
        and here's remembrance
arriving with the azure hiss of airmail letters:
        blanketed in black and white,

he's propped in wicker, the crescent of beach dissolving
        to sea behind him, the most
remote margin of land where on rare days it's possible
        to walk endlessly, it seems,

into breakers, the tide . . . Beside him, an ashen
        cyclamen. One failing stem
designs pure curve, the single bloom so like the shape
        of cormorants in flight

beyond tawny estuaries, beyond rollers in the bay
        striking out like the shoulders of
so many swimmers. At first his mortal glance seems empty,
        then it's clear the emptiness

is mine, that half-dreamt room is grief, a single
        creased syllable opening
to the circling of cormorants inviolate, beyond
        the coast of anything we know.

Adagio

Across Majestic Boulevard, *Steam Bath*
neons the snow to blue, and on her table
a blue cup steams, a rime of stale cream
circling its rim. Before finding the chipped case

behind the mirror, she waits for morning
the way an addict must wait, a little longer,
and studies the torn print on the wall—
lilies blurred to water stains, a woman

floating in a boat trailing fingers
in its wake. Someone rich. Someone gone.
Maybe a countess. She lets herself drift in the boat
warming thin translucent hands in coffee steam.

She's not a countess, only another girl
from the outer boroughs with a heroin habit as long
as the sea routes that run up and down the coast.
She's read all winter a life of Hart Crane, losing

her place, beginning again with Crane in a room
by the bridge, the East River, spending himself
lavishly. She's spent her night
circulating between piano bars and cabarets

where Greek sailors drink and buy her
cheap hotel champagne at 10 bucks a shot
before evaporating to another port on the map
of terra incognita the waterlilies chart

along her wall. The mantel is greened with
a chemical patina of sweat and time, and she can't
call any of this back. Hart Crane sways,
a bottle of scotch in one hand, his face plunged

inside the gramophone's tin trumpet, jazzed
to graceless oblivion. She rinses her face
in the basin, cold water, then turns to glance
across the boulevard where life's arranged

in all its grainy splendor. The steam bath sign
switches off with dawn, a few departing men
swathed in pea coats. The bath attendant climbs
as always to the roof, then opens the dovecote

to let his pigeons fly before descending to his berth.
They bank and curve toward the harbor that surrenders
to the sea. She knows Crane will leap
from the *Orizaba's* stern to black fathoms

of water, that one day she'll lock this room
and lose the key. The gas flame's yellow coronet
stutters and she rolls her stocking down at last
to hit the vein above her ankle, until carried forward

she thinks it's nothing but the velocity of the world
plunging through space, the tarnished mirror
slanted on the mantel showing a dove-gray sky
beginning to lighten, strangely, from within.

TWO

Edgemont: The Swans

Next, the dull silk thwack of an umbrella opening. No, that
was later, her grandmother's
hands & the umbrella smelled like some lost decade, like shelter—
camphor & lavender.
They're going to feed the swans, a long bus ride past
the wilderness of chrome
dinettes where soda jerks shimmy behind their blinding counters.
Tenements unpin themselves
from gray construction-paper sky dieseled to nothingness
by the bus's passage
to orange leaves pasting copper beeches in the park. There is

the door's pneumatic snap
behind them, then rain fuming the pavement, Indian summer
& couples loiter—
young men fatally cool in pointed shoes, leather jackets
wrapping the shoulders
of varnish-haired girls. Her grandmother holds
a sack of bread while
she kneels by the lake. Swans gloss toward shore & she sees
through her face in the shallows
by the sluice, a mask rippled over the bottom's plush ferment
of silt & leaves. Then silently,

the swans arrive opening & closing coral beaks, black tongues.
They cancel her reflection
with their cluster & jostle for crumbs. She knows about the gods,
how they come to earth sometimes
as swans. Dense mist rivulets snowy backs & her sweater is fog
when the slim necks arc over her

their soft, laddered clucking & what alien grace, the white weight
of swans leaving water
& for once she has no longing for the future, for beauty
beyond the trance of swans.
There's thunder & I know they all must leave the park for the
        heart's
violent destinations —
raptures & betrayals, departures & returns, a torrent
of stories bewildering

& arbitrary as any the gods might choose. In one,
war begins,
the swans are garroted with piano wire, a soldier
unraveling his skein
of private nightmares. Her grandmother saves the clipping.
Another has the girl
argue with her grandmother, take flight to suffer, almost
accidentally, her first kiss.
The darkened park. This utter stranger. But here the stories
blur until the soldier is
the stranger & the hands that tangle the girl's damp hair, tilt back
a long swan's neck, so rippling
transformed, she's reflected in that stricken human face trying
to lose itself over hers
in a ferment of white wings, sluice-water dousing park lights.

So many seasons' debris, where the crumbs she'd strewn
as a child vanish again,
chimerical as memory, & swans glide away carving
clear wakes in a timeless

still lake. I see a girl waiting for a bus.
Lightly, it's raining
on her grandmother's face so the umbrella opens its scent
& bus tickets stain
their hands with minute, indigo numbers that show the fare.

Visiting Hour

From the hospital solarium we watch row houses
change with evening down the avenue, the gardener

bending to red asters, his blond chrysanthemums.
Each day I learn more of the miraculous.

The gardener rocks on his heels and softly
Riva talks to me about the d.t.'s, her gin

hallucinations. The willow on the lawn
is bare, almost flagrant in the wind off

Baltimore harbor. She wants me to brush her hair.
Some mornings I'd hear her sing to herself

numbers she knew by heart
from nightclubs on the waterfront circuit.

I wondered if she watched herself dissolve
in the mirror as shadows flickered, then whispering

gathered. Floating up the airshaft
her hoarse contralto broke over "I Should Care,"

"Unforgettable," and in that voice
everything she remembered—the passage

from man to man, a sequence of hands
undressing her, letting her fall like the falling

syllables of rain she loves, of steam, those trains
and ships that leave. How she thought for years

a departure or a touch might console her, if only
for the time it takes luck to change, to drink

past memory of each stranger that faltered
over her body until her song was a current

of murmurs that drew her into sleep, into
the shapes of her fear. Insects boiling

from the drain, she tells me, a plague
of veiled nuns. Her hair snaps, electric

in the brush, long, the color of dust or rain
against a gunmetal sky. I saw her once, at the end

of a sullen July dusk so humid that the boys
loitering outside the Palace Bar & Grill

moved as if through vapor. She was reeling
in spike heels, her faded blue kimono.

They heckled her and showered her with pennies,
spent movie tickets. But she was singing.

That night I turned away and cursed myself
for turning. She holds a glass of water

to show her hands have grown more steady.
Look, she whispers, and I brush

and braid and the voices of visiting hour rise
then wind like gauze. The gardener's flowers nod,

pale in the arc lamps that rinse the factory boys
shooting craps as they always do down on

Sweet Air Avenue. I know they steam the dice
with breath for luck before they toss,

and over them the air shimmers the way still water
shimmers as gulls unfold like Riva's evening hands

across the sky, tremulous, endangered.

The Crossing, 1927

A floating city of substance, of ether
   and haze, the great liner crests and breaks through
      foam, streams of cold turquoise. On deck,
slippery, wet, deserted at six in the morning
   tall deck chairs rest in rows with their knees up

to their chins, I write on blue onionskin,
   a letter home. *My ninth day on the ocean*
      and we're almost to Havre. By noon
we'll be off the boat and on the train—
   Paris, the radiant destination.

I mouth its syllables, the name *Millay,* and think
   I'll change my name to *Violette.*
      Long before dawn, awake from restless half-sleep
I kept watch to see the sky rinse then pearl
   through the porthole, but no, and the whole ship

was sleeping, lingerie frothing from steamer trunks
   in watery light, cut iris on nightstands.
      Even the rats slumbering in the granary
or among the nervous legs of racehorses.
   Last night off starboard Laurence pointed toward

lighthouses, the Cornish coast, and I thought I'd die
   thinking of Tristan and Iseult, their story
      of rue and devotion and we were there
held in the same chill current, a couple
   with scotch on our breaths and I leaned over

the railing where waves churned, obscuring the glimmer
    of Cornwall then showing again the visible present
        streamed into myth, cold turquoise. Nine days at sea—
a floating city—and in the ship's grand ballroom
    the journey's last fête careened, everyone

chattering in French champagned beneath
    the chandeliers. Mademoiselle Simone's mynah slipped
        his gold leg chain and fluttered from table to table,
awkward on lopped wings shrieking *bloody pack*
    of knaves in dockside Limey English

so the orchestra cranked louder to drown
    him out but everyone was drunk and didn't care.
        Is it wrong, this craze for Europe,
this vast grand fling, all of us flooding from America,
    the crass and gaudy, towards what farther shore?

Beauty? A form of love or devotion?
    Thin arabesques of laughter, the sudden gash
        of a badly painted mouth. Outside
the deck dropped then crested like the roller coaster
    in Maine when I was a child—four stories tall—

the white roller coaster and through trees far below
    people strolled in straw hats and beyond the park
        the summer glitter of the same sea that frosted me
past midnight still warm and giddy from the ballroom.
    Salt mist crimped my hair, the blanket Laurence wrapped

around my shoulders. Tristan, wounded, crossed
    the Channel, maybe here, for Brittany and I
        shiver into the traveler's extravagant
elation veined with fear. Paris, the radiant destination.
    I wanted to see the day break over France

but the sun won't rise at all this morning
    because it's raining. Nine days at sea
        and this early I'm alone for once on deck
a minor jazz-age duenna without the rainbow-colored
    dress of scarves, no entourage of sloe-eyed flappers,

no flaming youths, only this solitary sway over
    cold marine depths, sunken crystal. The ship's
        a floating city of ether and haze awash
in bands of sea and sky that merge. Was there rain
    or sunlight when Tristan writhed with fever

waiting for the longboat which carried Iseult?
    Black sail, white sail, a confusion of sails.
        Tristan and Iseult each longing to be touched,
transformed, to be one and never, never,
    always that distance, that illusive

deceiving horizon. He suffers time the way
    a lover always will, a traveler, as if
        by having at last the loved one, as if
by merely arriving a completion takes place.
    The harrowed waves. Paris, the destination

an irreal embrace of starlight twenty-four hours
　　a day, white monuments gracing fragrant
　　　　boulevards. The cabin steward wants to know
if I'm cold but I don't care because the drop
　　of the deck is the white roller coaster

swinging over the sea, that stark
　　delicious vertigo and people
　　　　way below sipping lemonade with mint.
The steward shakes my shoulder, then with the bow
　　and flourish of a cabaret emcee

says, *Voilà, la terre de France,* and I stare
　　and stare a long time, not even thinking
　　　　and I don't care if it rains while the great liner
cruises these glorious, numbered hours.
　　The car, the car would hesitate then tilt as it lurched

to descend past hurtling signs—*Hold Your Hat,*
　　Don't Stand, at each turn, *Don't Let Go,*
and I know I will never arrive.

Aubade

Below the viaduct, the 5:05's stiff wind snares
the whole block in its backlash, and although
the morning fairly aches with promise, only
insomniacs are out, the million-dollar dreamers
orphaned by love's chameleon reversals.
What joins me to my neighbor is this

silent complicity: by flashlight I uproot
dandelions and crabgrass, while on his fire escape
he does calisthenics. A month ago he came home
to an empty flat and that emptiness turns
its dull blade inside his chest. Caught by the last
anemic sickle of moon, perhaps he thinks himself

more than half a man, but less than full.
This early the street's washed black and white,
jittery as a sixteen-millimeter reel. It's easy
to understand, at times like this, the sudden
desire to commend oneself into the hands
of sympathetic strangers who, in certain

transfiguring lights, wear the faces of husbands
and wives. And then there's the edgy allure
of the dangerous ones — that red-haired cashier
with an emerald piercing her nostril's flare,
or the carnival boy who tends the shooting booth —
those blind ducks with rings painted round

their necks. This business of being human
should not be such a lonely proposition. Maybe
I should drop my spade and stride

to my neighbor's alley, call out, *It is I,*
the one for whom you have been waiting.
Come down. Let us join our forces. Yes,

a brash tarantella through fireweed, the shattered
bottle glass. But I am not so bold, not nearly
so presuming. Instead I note the snail's
slimy progress and my neighbor touches toes
until the fog rolls down the hill like a memory
that wants losing. He performs deep knee bends

until he strikes a contract with himself
that gets him through his day, a deal not unlike
the one between earth and root, between
green pear and empty hand. My neighbor
crawls back through his window, his landing
sways its vacant iron grid, and above

the plummeting alley, a sleek gray seam of sky.
Pretty soon deals will go down all over the city.
The fruit vendor will appear singing strawberries
and watermelons. From their tanks, lobsters
in the seafood markets will wave pincers as if
imploring the broken factory clock that registers

9:99 in the morning, 0° even in the heart of summer.
Answer me. What am I to make of these signs?

Studies from Life

Soot-blackened, marble angels freeze
   their serpentine ascent above scattered women
      in the pews, net shopping bags beside them as

the priest drones Mass before an altar carbonized
   with Madrid's incessant traffic fumes. In stone,
      the Virgin rests her foot upon the serpent

coiling a benighted world, and tarnished
   in their reliquary, the hermit's fingers play
      no instrument but incensed air. Such a meager

gathering, yet here is the visionary beggar riding
   tissued layers of soiled garments, notebook
      in her hands, transcribing helplessly

her transport in a code of suns and doves'
   entrails, crouched seraphim. Because he believed
      the mad inhabited zones of heaven, El Greco

painted in asylums—the saint's blue arms
   raised in rapture truly modeled from the madman's
      supplications. Cries and rough whispers,

nuns' habits sweeping across stone floors, disturbing
   the stacks of charcoal studies. He found derangement
      spiritual. The cathedral font is dry today,

stained glass rattling the passage of Vespas
   and taxicabs. The stairway tumbles, Baroque,
      to the boulevard twitching with heat, gypsied with

cripples, the sots and marvelous dancing goats.
  In the Prado, Greco's attenuated aristocrat
    buys his way to grace beside a Virgin transfigured—

the Resurrection. What Calvary in the model's mind
  built that cathedraled radiance of her glance,
    so matte and dense and holy? They're everywhere

in these vivid streets living parallel
  phantasmic cities that shimmer and burn among
    swirling crowds along the esplanade—tangoing couples

dappled under trees, the fortune-tellers
  and summer girls like dropped chiffon scarves
    sipping their turquoise infusions, planetary liqueurs

sticky with umbrellas. They chatter through
  a dwarf's frantic homily of curses. Simply
    a ripple the crowd absorbs, but where is the saint

from the plains' walled city the tourists
  come to find? *Oh, she is broken on the wheel,*
    milled into dust. She is atomized to history's

dry footnotes. Here is the sleek plane's vapor,
  the speed-blind train, and there the fragrant secrets
    inside fine leather. Still, the painter shows the beggar's

empty bowl, irradiated shades, these gaseous figures
  writhing upward, hands knotting tremulous prayers.
    And the mouths, the mouths. . . Such hollow caverns

that plumb what depths of human pain, or is it
     ecstasy's abandon? Past a twilight the color of sighs
          on the street made numinous with restaurant lights,

he is there, the man kneeling before a shopfront's
     iron grille. Facing, rapt, a silk-swathed mannequin,
          he's chanting litanies in a perfumed tongue

of numerals, some unearthly lexicon. And if we could
     translate, we might hear how the saint dwells
          perpetual, the form of this hunger within.

Utopia Parkway

after Joseph Cornell's *Penny Arcade*
Portrait of Lauren Bacall, 1945–46

Marble steps cascade like stereopticon
frames of quays along the Seine he's ready
to descend, a folio beneath his arm
or yellowed pages wreathed in the aura of French,
a cache of star maps and movie stills, Lauren Bacall.

Parisian breezes siphon off into slight vacuums
left in air by the passage of young men
wheeling racks of suits and dresses toward
the Garment District. New York and the twilit
Public Library steps where each instant spins

a galaxy of signs—the flushed marquees
and newsboys' shouts fold into hoarse cries, street vendors
of former times when parrots picked fortune cards
from drawers beneath their hurdy-gurdy cages
outside Coney Island's Penny Arcade. Toward

Times Square, streaming taillights weave nets of connections
carmine as Bacall's lips ticked pout in *Screenplay*
Magazine, and the whole bedazzled city's
a magnificent arcade one might arrange in a cabinet,
those amusement-park contraptions worked by coins

or tinted wooden balls traveling runways
to set into motion compartment
after compartment, a symphony of sight and sound
into fantasy, into the streets of New York through
Oriental skies, until the balls come to rest

in their tray releasing a shower of prizes:
a milliner's illuminated display of hats,
the stamp hat tilted over Bacall's arched eyebrows, filings
spread across the inspector's desk, her sullen gaze.
On Utopia Parkway, in his workshop, Bacall's

dossier's lain for months untouched among springs
and dolls' heads, ballerinas arcing through
charted celestial spheres, that music.
Hoagy Carmichael's heard offstage as he threads
the rush-hour crowd. A typist's crooked stocking seams

recall with affection the actress on her way up—
the modeling jobs, ushering in New York. The box will work
by a rolling ball wandering afield into childhood,
an insight into the lives of countless young women
who never knew, may never know, any other home

than the plainest of furnished rooms, a drab hotel.
The drama of a room by lamplight, hotel neon
in *To Have and Have Not.* Carmichael's "Hong Kong Blues,"
blue glass like the night-blue of early silent films—
an atmosphere of cabaret songs, "How Little We Know."

Fog, the boat scenes, and each compartment becomes
a silver screen. Offstage music, and now we hear
the music in Cornell's eternity as the actress
takes her place among the constellations,
Cygnus, the Pleiades, one of the Graces.

Gateway to Manhattan

Someone's saying it's almost time for the ambulance.
Then there's your own shocked face
in the Public Bathroom's mirror, already underwater,
the woman curled at your feet, foam speckling her lips.
Beyond these sinks, toward blind pavilions
escalators lunge briefcases, scented fur coats
conveyed above mental patients set loose upon the town.
Counterfeit daylight thrums the upper platform's
bland heaven. Familiar numbered streets erase themselves —
your ride uptown — 14th, 23rd, 42nd, counting into the concourse
swarmed with zero-hour losers, newsprint, incense,
that Haitian lynx cooing her rich patois, hawking charms for
    nightmare's
hexed recurrent voodoo. Counterfeit daylight.

The *No* clenched inside. On the tiles, the woman whose throat
is ringed with bandanas, whose collapse is a stain you want
to step around. Shove your hands deep inside your pockets
and make like you're cool about the few decisions away she lays
beneath the cascade of endless running faucets. Someone's
calling for an ambulance. Where is your room, lucid
sunlight fanning rooftops? Where is the subway stop
named *Esperanza*? No, that was another country.
Hope, safe haven against the riptide's snarling wake. A heaven
vast, impersonal. So where are the angels of Reckoning
and Assuagement to hold this woman's hand, thin fingers
splayed against the tiles beneath her many coats?
And you're part of this, Doll, by the indifferent turn
of an ankle, the glance casually averted. Let's say
once she believed in human goodness among these blind pavilions.

This woman. Lie down with her, nestle your face
in retch and tremor, her rank hair. Palm her temples.
Lie down in the whir of roofs lifting away as you knew
they always must, clamorous pauses between marquees and
    parking lots
filled with an ascension of pigeons. Shall those who'll
die, like her, so publicly, hear the underneath of plosive secret
    voices?
How up and down the island buildings bulge and sob, the great
tailor's shears above Varick Street clipping endlessly the thread
that holds all of this together, these partial stories overheard:

          Chestnuts steaming on a brazier,
yes . . .
     Play a tenspot,
             Silverice in the eighth . . .
The 5:12,
      missing that, the 5:28 . . .
We always liked . . .
         The mind has precincts of pain, exiles
within the precincts of pain . . .

So, listen now with her to this broken wake of commuters
safe in their passage, always passing. And who bears responsibility?
Only angels of Fraud and Dissembling
tinsel the Strip tonight, a ceaseless run of water
from busted taps telling how it felt as she let go,
fingers loosening, her many clothes unfurling. Dante's Grove
of Suicides, you think. But no. Allusions break down.
She'd have nothing but contempt for you, guilty and standing here
long past the last train, waiting for the police sweep,

waiting for the clamp on the wrist, concrete sweating against
      your forehead.
It's almost time for the sirens to begin, the shaking,
a trembling from within.

42nd, 23rd, 14th counting backward, so when at last
the Haitian arrives to press earth into your hands, a rubble
of bone and charms, you'll go down on your knees, willing to pay,
and keep on paying. Wasn't this exactly what you wanted?

Magical Thinking

A woman, after an absence of many years, returns
   to her old neighborhood and finds it a little more
      burned, more abandoned. Through rooftop aerials

the stadium's still visible where the boys of summer
   spun across the diamond and some nights she'd hear
      strikes and pop flies called through the open windows

of the rooms she shared with a man she thought
   she loved. All that summer, she watched
      across the street the magician's idiot son

paint over and over the Magic & Costume Shop's
   intricate portico—all frets and scallops, details
      from another century. The more he painted though

the more his sheer purity of attention seemed
   to judge her own life as frayed somehow and wrong.
      Daily the son worked until the city swerved

toward night's dizzy carnival with moons
   and swans afloat in neon over the streets.
      One evening she saw the magician's trick bouquet

flower at the curb while he filled his car.
   He folded the multicolored scarves, then
      caged the fabulous disappearing pigeons.

It is a common human longing to want utterly
   to vanish from one life and arrive transformed
      in another. When the man came home, he'd

touch her shoulders, her neck, but each touch
   discovered only the borders of her solitude.
      As a child in that neighborhood she'd believed

people were hollow and filled with quiet music, that
   if she were hurt deeply enough she would break
      and leave only a blue scroll of notes.

At first when he hit her, her face burned.
   Far off the stadium lights crossed the cool
      green diamond and burnished cobwebs swaying

on the ceiling. Then she became invisible,
   so when the doctor leaned over and asked
      her name all she could think of were her dresses

thrown from the window like peonies exploding
   to bloom in the clear dark air. No music—
      merely a rose haze through her lids, something

ticking in her head like a metronome
   in a parlor, dusty and arid with steam heat.
      How many lives she'd passed through to find

herself, an aging woman in black, before the locked
   and empty shop. So much sleight of hand, the years
      simply dissolving. Again she hears the crowd,

a billow of applause rippling across the brilliant
   diamond, across the mysterious passage
      of time and the failure of sorrow to pass away.

Utsuroi

Of course there's the rose
tranced across sun-warmed tile,

but also the soft tattoo
of newsprint along a commuter's palm,

the flush of a motel sign the instant
it signals No Vacancy. I have always loved

these moments of delicate transition:
waking alone in a borrowed house

to a slim meridian of dawn barring
the pillow before the cool breeze,

a curtain of rain on the iron steps, rain
laving lawn chairs arranged

for a conversation finished days ago.
The Japanese call this *utsuroi*,

a way of finding beauty at the point
it is altered, so it is not the beauty

of the rose, but its evanescence
which tenders the greater joy.

Beneath my hands the cat's thick fur
dapples silver, the slant of afternoon.

How briefly they flourish then turn,
exalted litanies in the rifts

between milliseconds, time enough for a life
to change, and change utterly.

The magnesium flash of headlights
passing backlit the boy's face

in my novel—the heroine's epiphany
and she knows she is leaving, a canopy

of foliage surrounds his dark hair
whispering *over, over*—that sweet rending.

Nothing linear to this plot, simply
the kaleidoscopic click and shift

of variations undone on the instant:
evening as it vanishes gilds

the chambermaid's thin blond hair
in her hotel window and she thinks

I could die now, and it would be enough.
Long beyond nightfall, after the café's closing

the waiters slide from their jackets and set
places for themselves, paper lanterns blowing

in the trees, leaf shapes casting and recasting
their fugitive spell over the tables,

over the traffic's sleek sussurrus.

~ THREE

Cubism, Barcelona

So easily you fall to sleep, the room a cage of rain,
the wallpaper's pinstripe floral another rift
between us, this commerce of silences and mysteries
called marriage, but that's not what this is about.

It's this wet balcony, filigreed, this rusty fan of spikes
the pensione's installed against thieves and this weather—

needling rain that diminuendoes into vapor, fog
dragging its cat's belly above the yellow spikes
of leaves, the hungry map the hustlers make stitching through
the carnival crowd below, and I'm thinking of Picasso's

early work—an exhibit of childhood notebooks, a *Poetics'*
margins twisting with doves and bulls and harlequins. Your face,

our friends', the sullen milling Spaniards, repeated canvases
of faces dismantled, fractured so as to contain
the planar flux of human expression—boredom to lust
and fear, then rapture and beyond. He was powerless,

wasn't he, before all that white space? I mean he had to
fill it in, and I can fill in the blank space of this room

between you and me, between me and the raucous promenade,
with all the rooms and galleries I've known, now so wantonly
painting themselves across this room, this night, the way
I extend my hand and the paseo, foreign beyond my fingertips,

dissolves to a familiar catastrophe of façades, the angles
of walls and ceilings opening all the way to the waterfront

where the standard naked lightbulb offers its crude flower
of electricity to blue the dark abundant hair a woman
I could have been is brushing, a torn shade rolled up to see
the bird vendor's cat upon his shoulder or, at some other stage

in their pursuit, the same French sailor I see drunkenly
courting the queen dolled up in bedsheet and motorcycle chain,

some drag diva strung out on something I can't name, something
kicking like this vicious twin inside who longs to walk
where guidebooks say not to, who longs to follow beyond all
common sense, that childhood love of terror propelling us

through funhouses and arcades, mother of strange beauty and faith.
But it's only chill rain that gathers in my palm, the empty

terra-cotta pots flanking the balcony. Rain and the ache
in my hands today, those off-tilt Gaudis queasily spelling
the tilt from port to port any life describes: Boston's damp cold
and we're stuffing rags again in broken windows, that condemned

brownstone on harshly passionate—Mr. Lowell—Marlborough
    Street
where our feet skimmed, polished black across the floor,

damp, the tattered hems of trousers. Simply trying like always
to con our way to some new dimension. And weren't we glamorous?
Oh, calendar pages riffling in the artificial wind
of some offscreen fan, a way to show life passing, the blurred

collage of images we collect to show everything and nothing
has changed. But I want to talk about the swans of Barcelona

this afternoon in the monastery pool, battered palms
and small bitter oranges smashed against pavement stones.
And those swans, luxurious and shrill by turns. It's not swans
that arrest me now — only this sailor staggering on the paseo

fisting the air between him and the queen, shouting *je sens, je sens,*
but he isn't able to say what he feels any more than I understand

how it is that perspective breaks down, that the buried life
wants out on sleepless nights amidst these coils of citizens,
a carnival dragon snaking, sodden, through the trees above them.
I know. I know, there's got to be more than people ruthlessly

hurricaned from port to port. I know tomorrow is a prayer
that means hope, that now you breathe softly, sleeping face

rent by sooted shadows the thief's grille throws while you're
turned into whatever dream you've made of these curious days
filled with cockatoos and swans, the endless rain.
Things get pretty extreme, then tomorrow little blades

of grass will run from silver into green
down the esplanade where a waiter places

ashtrays on the corners of tablecloths
to keep them firmly anchored.

The drag queen will be hustling, down on her knees
in the subway, a few exotic feathers twisting in the wind.

But it won't be me, Jack. It won't be me.

Counting in Chinese

Past midnight, September, and the moon dangles
mottled like a party lantern about to erupt
in smoke. The first leaves in the gutter eddy,
deviled by this wind that's traveled years,

whole latitudes, to find me here believing
I smell the fragrance of mock orange. For weeks
sometimes, I can go without thinking of you.
Crumpled movie handbills lift then skitter

across the pavement. They advertise the one
I've just seen — "Drunken Angel" — Kurosawa's
early film of occupied Japan, the Tokyo slums
an underworld of makeshift market stalls

and shacks where Matsu, the consumptive gangster,
dances in a zoot suit to a nightclub's swing band.
The singer mimes a parody of Cab Calloway
in Japanese. And later, as Matsu leans coughing

in a dance-hall girl's rented room, her painted
cardboard puppet etches shadows on the wall
that predict his rival's swift razor
and the death scene's slow unfurling, how

he falls endlessly it seems through a set
of doors into a heaven of laundry: sheets
on the line, the obis and kimonos stirring
with his passage. And all of this equals

a stark arithmetic of choices, his fate
the final sum. Why must it take so long
to value what's surrendered so casually?
I see you clearly now, the way you'd wait

for me, flashy beneath the Orpheum's
rococo marquee in your Hong Kong hoodlum's
suit, that tough-guy way you'd flick
your cigarette when I was late. You'd consult

the platinum watch, the one you'd lose
that year to poker. I could find again our room
above the Lucky Life Café, the cast-iron district
of sweatshop lofts. But now the square's deserted

in this small midwestern town, sidewalks
washed in the vague irreal glow of shopwindows,
my face translucent in the plate glass.
I remember this the way I'd remember a knife

against my throat: that night, after
the overdose, you told me to count, to calm
myself. You put together the rice-paper lantern
and when the bulb heated the frame it spun

shadows—dragon, phoenix, dragon and phoenix
tumbling across the walls where the clothes
you'd washed at the sink hung drying on
a nailed cord. The mock orange on the sill

blessed everything in that room
with its plangent useless scent. Forgive me.
I am cold and draw my sweater close. I discover
that I'm counting, out loud, in Chinese.

Carnival

Barcelona

Sure the advertisements are full of advice. They beseech
      everyone to get drunk or go
on vacation, to keep journeying to fill the wrenched vacancy,
      keep moving forward to find out

what's behind us—old news. By now the bird vendors are out
      dealing cockatoos and jeweled finches,
ringed pigeons, corrosively iridescent with morning.
      It's true the architecture's complex,

but sometimes I get fed up with swallowing diesel
      and cruising around in someone else's idea
of the good life. So here I am counting the hairs I've lost,
      while on the promenade people air

their ocelots beneath balconies festooned with streamers,
      confetti staining a turbaned sheik
three stories high bowing over a couple who've been up all night.
      The woman rolls a cigarette, blows smoke

while the man, wearing a lush's face, looks down at the table,
      hands over his eyes. Think I'll just
stay here to contemplate the defects of my own character,
      the pressed tin ceiling a topographical map

tattooed across the brain—my little piece of the universe.
      I know the clubs are full of parrots
with fortunes to tell, fat women in magenta tutus flashing
      the vast marble expanses

of their backs and all of them saying, "Where you from?"
  Singapore, Bali, the Republic
of Wherever I Want to Be From. The pipes screech their burden
  and last night that wrecked chanteuse

from 1936 told me the story of Barcelona's anarchists, three times
  how they shot her nephew,
nine years old, for stealing a chair. You see he had it wrong.
  He should have destroyed the chair.

A joke's no laughing matter here. Maybe I should dye my hair,
  book up the coast to Marseilles,
down to Marrakesh. I want to say there's time. That I have
  no regrets. Maybe I'll take a stroll,

drop a coin and talk to someone about the way life seems
  a dream of anarchy on highways, through masques
and arcades, the jittery palpitations, torrents of which
  the present is composed. The carnival resumes,

Ferris wheels slicing circles in the sky. Pipes burst
  an explosion of birds. So, I'm leaning over
the railing counting the pickpockets, addressing you,
  the abstract "you" that's the sum of everyone

I've known or lost or longed for. You know what I mean.
  What I want you to tell me
is how are we to fit between these palaces of justice
  and the waterfront's

bedraggled carnival? Or that ramshackle museum
           with cracked and muzzy skylights,
pots carefully arranged to catch the rain? Artifacts,
           I swear to you, disappeared before my eyes.

Frugal Repasts

After the ribboning fever of interstate, after freight yards
& tinsel-towns, through the cranked-up mojo of radio signals,
through the moteled drift of nonsleep, comes the arms crossed

over the chest, the mind's blind odometer clicking backward,
comes sifting over years the musk of those opened crates spilling

into that room, the abandoned building. Just me & him. Comes
the torn Army jacket & Detroit voice, dusky, the sweat-grayed
T-shirt. A cup of snow-water melted on the ledge. No light—

simply candles pooled in wax across the floor, nothing more, but
those crates of rose crystal, hot out the backdoor of some swank shop.

While shadows flickered bare lathes, while he spasmed
the strung-out toss of too much hunger, too long, I set out
the beautiful *idea* of feast. Rose crystal plates & saucers

lined the mattress's thin margin of floor, guttering flames,
those teacup rims. Just me & him, that nameless jacket,

olive drab. I wanted to catch the cries, the ragged breath, how
we used to say come the revolution we'd survive anything, anything,
& condemned to that frugal repast we were, somehow, free.

Snow-water melted in the cup rinsed his forehead, that pure
juncture of clavicle & shoulder. Better this immersion

than to live untouched. I wanted to be the cup & flame,
I wanted to be the cure, the hand that held the river back
that would break us, as in time, we broke each other. Wait.

Not yet. While great newspresses crashed over next day's
headlines, while alley cats stalled beyond the wrenched police-lock

in a frieze of ferocious longing, his arms clenched the flawless
ache of thigh, damp curls. No clinic till break of day to break
the stream of fever I rocked with him toward the story I told

as a girl: the perfect city, luminous in the back of the radio,
jazz turned down so low it ghosted improvisations that let me fly

immune above skyscrapers, the endless gleaming arguments
of streets. I set out the platter, a delicate tureen & then
we *were* spark & fever, all frequencies tuned until

that piss-poor stinking room seemed shouldered through torn
    skyline.
Through spark & fever, shouldered beyond the folly of others

set adrift: the room of the girl who bends to gas flame deciding
coffee or suicide, beyond Roxbury's Emperor of Byzantium
alone on his Murphy-bed throne, tinfoil minarets & domes.

Condemned & oddly free, my hand following his ribs' dark curve,
the ridge of muscle there & there. James, what's the use?

After the broken arpeggios of all these years, comes this waking,
this stooping to the gas flame, comes the learning & relearning
through the long open moan of highway going on toward

a stream of crimson lifting away from the horizon. I wanted to
be the hand that held back the river, destiny. Comes this new day

cruelly, unspeakably rich, as that drenched grisaille of morning
came pouring then over blackened wicks, over all that crystal
fired empty & clean. Better this immersion than to live untouched.

Abacus

No grand drama, only Chinatown's incendiary glow,
me returning to the old delinquent thrill of us

passing through this jimmied door, the herbalist's
shop gone broke & latticed with accordion grille.

Are these faces of ours oddly gentled, First Husband,
as evening's verge spills over bad-news gang-boys

filling vestibules with their bored sangfroid, over
old women smoothing newsprint sheets for carp steamed

to feathers of flesh? Two doors down, the gold-toothed
Cantonese lifts her tray of pastries streaming

red characters for sweet lotus, bitter melon, those
for fortune, grief, for marriage & rupture.

In my wallet, the torn wedding picture sleeps —
your brilliantine & sharkskin, my black-brimmed hat,

a cluster of glass cherries. Too young. Words roil
to calligraphy above us, cold as the dawn

your second wife wakes to, day-old rice then scorched
fluorescence through sweatshops, through bobbins

& treadles, the 6¢ piecework. When it's time,
we'll exchange a formal kiss in the whorling updraft

of burnt matches & apothecary labels, gang graffiti
slashed upon the walls. Why return to this empty shop

where I'd meet you sometimes after-hours over poker,
men chanting numbers in a sinuous grammar of 40-watt light

& smoke? Not much here now, a few drafty rooms, broken
drams of pungent White Flower Oil you'd rub my feet with,

bruised from dancing six sets a night between the star acts.
Not much, but what I choose to shape sleepless nights

far from here, when I'm diaphanous, engulfed again
by Chinatown's iron lintels, the hiss & spill of neon fog,

heliotrope & jade unrolled against the pavement I'd walk
in filmy stockings, the impossible platform shoes. As if

I might find her here again, my lost incarnation fallen
from the opulent emptiness of nightclubs, those

restaurants tuxedoed in their hunger. No one could
translate such precise Esperanto. And so we linger

tiny, surviving protagonists briefly safe here
from the crowd's ruthless press, a fanfare

of taxis polishing the avenues. Whenever next
I meet you, I'll meet you here in the harsh

auroral radiance of the squad car's liquid lights.
Things have never been so essential. I have seen

businesses fold & open like paper lilies, & men
leave for Hong Kong, then return to lie down

again in crowded rooms, the way each of us
lies down with a lacquered maze of corridors

& places where those once loved unbearably wear
strangers' faces. You run your hand through the hair

you've dyed black to hide the gray & out
on the street, sweet-faced vandals arabesque

caught in a rain of trinkets, green cards, the lucky
one-eyed jacks. Beneath my fingers, the twisted

braille of hearts & knives incised upon
the counter works its spell until the herbalist

takes up his abacus once more to commence
the sum of unguents, of healing roots,

a measure of time, a calculation beyond all worth.

Lost Fugue for Chet

Chet Baker, Amsterdam, 1988

A single spot slides the trumpet's flare then stops
   at that face, the extraordinary ruins thumb-marked
with the hollows of heroin, the rest chiaroscuroed.
   Amsterdam, the final gig, canals & countless

stone bridges arc, glimmered in lamps. Later this week
   his Badlands face, handsome in a print from thirty
years ago, will follow me from the obituary page
   insistent as windblown papers by the black cathedral

of St. Nicholas standing closed today: pigeon shit
   & feathers, posters swathing tarnished doors, a litter
of syringes. Junkies cloud the gutted railway station blocks
   & dealers from doorways call *coca, heroina,* some throaty

foaming harmony. A measured inhalation, again
   the sweet embouchure, metallic, wet stem. Ghostly,
the horn's improvisations purl & murmur
   the narrow *strasses* of *Rosse Buurt,* the district rife

with purse-snatchers, women alluring, desolate, poised
   in blue windows, Michelangelo boys, hair spilling
fluent running chords, mares' tails in the sky green
   & violet. So easy to get lost, these cavernous

brown cafés. Amsterdam, & its spectral fogs, its
   bars & softly shifting tugboats. He builds once more
the dense harmonic structure, the gabled houses.
   Let's get lost. Why court the brink & then step back?

After surviving, what arrives? So what's the point
    when there are so many women, creamy callas with single
furled petals turning in & in upon themselves
    like variations, nights when the horn's coming

genius riffs, metal & spit, that rich consuming rush
    of good dope, a brief languor burnishing
the groin, better than any sex. Fuck Death.
    In the audience, there's always this gaunt man, cigarette

in hand, black Maserati at the curb, waiting,
    the fast ride through mountain passes, descending with
no rails between asphalt & precipice. Inside, magnetic
    whispering *take me there, take me*. April, the lindens

& horse chestnuts flowering, cold white blossoms
    on the canal. He's lost as he hears those inner voicings,
a slurred veneer of chords, molten, fingering
    articulate. His glance below Dutch headlines, the fall

"accidental" from a hotel sill. Too loaded. What do you do
    at the brink? Stepping back in time, I can only
imagine the last hit, lilies insinuating themselves
    up your arms, leaves around your face, one hand vanishing

sabled to shadow. The newsprint photo & I'm trying
    to recall names, songs, the sinuous figures, but facts
don't matter, what counts is out of pained dissonance,
    the sick vivid green of backstage bathrooms, out of

broken rhythms—and I've never forgotten, never—
   this is the tied-off vein, this is 3 a.m. terror
thrumming, this is the carnation of blood clouding
   the syringe, you shaped *summer rains across the quays*

of Paris, flame suffusing jade against a girl's
   dark ear. From the trumpet, pawned, redeemed, pawned again
you formed one wrenching blue arrangement, a phrase endlessly
   complicated as that twilit dive through smoke, applause,

the pale haunted rooms. Cold chestnuts flowering April
   & you're falling from heaven in a shower of eighth notes
to the cobbled street below & foaming dappled horses
   plunge beneath the still green waters of the Grand Canal.

Vita Brevis

Houseboats roll soft with morning's thin drizzle,
    gypsy colors muted
  as we pass to wander the arboretum's
intricate chill paths,
    oval disks naming trees in Dutch,
      the familiar grown

  exotic in this city built on land
      that is sea, where
    our reflections merge with buildings floating
upside-down. A coverlet
    of ground mist wraps our ankles, so we seem,
      for a moment, nearly

  aerial, incorporeal within the distant
      sough of foghorns,
    then the museum's zones of pure atmosphere, galleries
of trompe l'oeils,
    convex interiors, the underwater hush
      of voices. Rain steady

  against the skylights' frosted lozenges dapples
      floors and walls, until
    outside is inside and we move among the lit
chambers of genre paintings
    lavish with detail, small parables
      of *vanitas* — dust

  circling the goblet's rim, half-empty, flies
      swimming the burst pear's
    nectar. Excess and transience: even in Vermeer,

a girl bending to
        her lustrous task weighs palmfuls of pearls,
            the Last Judgment pinned

    behind her in aquatint. Books crumble from leather
            bindings, and time glazes
        the fish's iridescent scales—decay so palpable
it stains the clearing sky
        of afternoon, late in this violent century,
            in time of plague.

    I've seen the shadow cross over young men, clustered
            addicts in parks
        where bronzed explorers survey the Atlantic's
cold immensities, measured
        in parchments like these cartographer's fancies, a world
            more mysterious,

    perhaps more richly imagined. The wing of afternoon
            tilts duskward, ochered in
        brief splendor and all around the tender regard
of countless saints
        and virgins. The closing hour signals and we enter
            again our fragile lives,

    bridges and boulevards webbed overhead
            with trolley wires,
        a host of tiny colored lights electrified
like constellations
        to conjure time's strange torque, the instant pulsing
            to a life's span

as we turn once more toward each shining
arborvitae, toward
evening gardens drenched in the radiant
calm hue of chamomile,
this illusion of a universe,
a proffered gift.

Hospice

Frayed cables bear perilously the antiquated lift,
all glass and wrought-iron past each apartment floor
like those devices for raising and lowering
angels of rescue in medieval plays. Last night
the stairwell lamps flickered off and I was borne up
the seven floors in darkness, the lift a small lit

cage where I thought of you, of the Catholic souls
we envisioned once, catechism class, the saint
in her moment of grace transfigured as she's engulfed
in flames. The lift shivered to a halt above the shaft
and I was afraid for a moment to open the grille,
wanting that suspension again, the requiemed hum

of one more city going on without me — Cockney girls
with violet hair swirling among the businessmen
and movie ushers of Soho, sullen in their jackets.
All of them staving off as long as they can
the inevitable passing away, that bland euphemism
for death. But I can't shake this from my mind:

your face with its hollows against hospital linen.
Newark's empty asylum wings opened again this year
for the terminal cases. Each day another
strung-out welfare mother, the street-corner romeos
we used to think so glamorous, all jacked-up
on two-buck shots. It was winter when I last was home

and my mother found you on her endless dietician's
rounds, her heavy ring of keys. It was winter
when I saw you, Loretta, who taught me to curse

in Italian, who taught me to find the good vein
in the blue and yellow hours of our sixteenth year
among deep nets of shadows dragged through evening, a surf

of trees by the railway's sharp cinders. Glittering
like teen-dream angels in some corny AM song,
buoyed by whatever would lift us above the smoldering
asphalt, the shingled narrow houses, we must
have felt beyond all damage. Still what damage carried you
all these years beyond the fast season of loveliness

you knew before the sirens started telling your story
all over town, before the habit stole
the luster from your movie-starlet hair.
Little sister, the orderlies were afraid to
touch you. Tonight, the current kicks the lights
back on and there's the steady moan of the lift's

descent, the portion of what's left of this day
spread before me—stockings drying on the sill, the cool
shoulders of milk bottles—such small domestic salvations.
There was no deus ex machina for you, gone now
this half year, no blazing escape, though how many times

I watched you rise again, and again from the dead:
that night at the dealer's on Orange Street, stripping
you down, overdosed and blanched against the green linoleum,
ice and saline. I slapped you until
the faint flower of your breath clouded the mirror.
In those years I thought death was a long blue hallway

you carried inside, a curtain lifting at the end
in the single window's terrible soft breeze where
there was always a cashier ready to take your
last silver into her gloved hands, some dicey, edgy game.
Beneath the ward clock's round dispassionate face
there was nothing so barren in the sift from minute

to absolute minute, a slow-motion atmosphere dense
as the air of medieval illuminations with demons
and diaphanous beings. I only wished then
the cancellation of that hungering that turns us
toward the mortal arms of lovers or highways
or whatever form of forgetfulness we choose.

Your breath barely troubled the sheets, eyes closed,
perhaps already adrift beyond the body, twisting
in a tissue of smoke and dust over Jersey's
infernal glory of cocktail lounges and chemical plants,
the lonely islands of gas stations lining the turnpike
we used to hitch toward the shore, a moment

I want back tonight—you and me on the boardwalk,
the casino arcade closed around its pinball machines
and distorting mirrors. Just us among sea serpents,
and the reckless murmur of the sea. Watching stars
you said you could almost believe the world arranged

by a design that made a kind of sense. That night
the constellations were so clear it was easy
to imagine some minor character borne up
beyond judgment into heaven, rendered purely

into light. Loretta, this evening washes
over my shoulders, this provisional reprieve.

I've been telling myself your story for months
and it spreads in the dusk, hushing the streets, and there
you are in the curve of a girl's hand as she lights
her cigarette sheltered beneath the doorway's plaster
cornucopia. Listen, how all along the avenue trees
are shaken with rumor of this strange good fortune.

Black Mare

It snakes behind me, this invisible chain gang—
the aliases, your many faces peopling

that vast hotel, the past. What did we learn?
Every twenty minutes the elevated train,

the world shuddering beyond
the pane. It was never warm enough in winter.

The walls peeled, the color of corsages
ruined in the air. Sweeping the floor,

my black wig on the chair. I never meant
to leave you in that hotel where the voices

of patrons long gone seemed to echo in the halls,
a scent of spoiled orchids. But this was never

an elegant hotel. The iron fretwork of the El
held each room in a deep corrosive bloom.

This was the bankrupt's last chance, the place
the gambler waits to learn his black mare's

leg snapped as she hurtled toward the finish line.

How did we live? Your face over my shoulder
was the shade of mahogany in the speckled

mirror bolted to the wall. It was never warm.
You arrived through a forest of needles,

the white mist of morphine, names for sleep
that never came. My black wig unfurled

across the battered chair. Your arms circled me
when I stood by the window. Downstairs

the clerk who read our palms broke the seal
on another deck of cards. She said you're my fate,

my sweet annihilating angel, every naked hotel room
I've ever checked out of. There's nothing

left of that, but even now when night pulls up
like a limousine, sea-blue, and I'm climbing the stairs,

keys in hand, I'll reach the landing and
you're there—the one lesson I never get right.

Trains hurtled by, extinguished somewhere
past the bend of midnight. The shuddering world.

Your arms around my waist. I never meant to leave.

.⸴ .⸴ .⸴

Of all of that, there's nothing left but a grid
of shadows the El tracks throw over the street,

the empty lot. Gone, the blistered sills,
voices that rilled across each wall. Gone,

the naked bulb swinging from the ceiling,
that chicanery of light that made your face

a brief eclipse over mine. How did we live?
The mare broke down. I was your fate, that

yellow train, the plot of sleet, through dust
crusted on the pane. It wasn't warm enough.

What did we learn? All I have left of you
is this burnt place on my arm. So, I won't

forget you even when I'm nothing but
small change in the desk clerk's palm, nothing

but the pawn ticket crumpled in your pocket,
the one you'll never redeem. Whatever I meant

to say loses itself in the bend of winter
toward extinction, this passion of shadows falling

like black orchids through the air. I never meant
to leave you there by the pane, that

terminal hotel, the world shuddering with trains.

The Only World

ONE

Chiffon

Fever, down-right dirty sweat
   of a heat-wave in May turning everyone
      pure body. Back of knee, cleavage, each hidden

crease, nape of neck turning steam. Deep
   in last night's vast factory, the secret
      wheels that crank the blue machinery

of weather bestowed this sudden cool,
   the lake misting my morning walk, this
      vacant lot lavish with iris — saffron,

indigo, bearded and striated, a shock
   of lavender clouds among shattered brick
      like cumulus that sail the tops of high-rises

clear evenings. Surprising as the iris garden
   I used to linger in, a girl distant from me
      now as a figure caught in green glass,

an oasis gleamed cool with oval plaques
   naming blooms Antoinette, My Blue Sunset,
      Festival Queen. This morning's iris frill

damp as fabulous gowns after dancing,
   those rummage sale evening gowns church ladies
      gave us another hot spring, 1967.

JoAnn who'd soon leave school, 14, pregnant,
   Valerie with her straightened bouffant hair.
      That endless rooftop season before the panic

and sizzle, the torched divided cities,
    they called me *cousin on the light side.*
        Camphorous, awash in rusty satin rosettes,

in organdy, chiffon, we'd practice
    girl group radio-hits—Martha Reeves
        but especially Supremes—JoAnn vamping

Diana, me and Valerie doing Flo and Mary's
    background moans, my blond hair pinned
        beneath Jo's mother's Sunday wig.

The barest blue essence of Evening in Paris
    scented our arms. We perfected all the gestures,
        JoAnn's liquid hands sculpting air,

her fingers' graceful cupping, wrist turning,
    palm held flat, "Stop in the Name of Love,"
        pressing against the sky's livid contrails,

a landscape flagged with laundry, tangled
    aerials and billboards, the blackened
        railway bridges and factories ruinous

in their fumes. Small hand held against the flood
    of everything to come, the savage drifting years.
        I'm a lucky bitch. Engulfed in the decade's riotous

swells, that lovely gesture, the dress, plumage
    electrifying the fluid force of that young body.
        She was gang-raped later that year. The rest,

as they say, *is history.* History.
　　When I go back I pore the phone book for names
　　　　I'll never call. Peach Pavilion, Amethyst

Surprise. *Cousin on the light side.* Bend
　　to these iris, their piercing ambrosial
　　　　essence, the heart surprised, dark and bitter.

Red Velvet Jacket

It's almost Biblical driving this midnight burning highway
past South Bronx exits
with the names of streets once known, where torched cars
spiral columns
acetylene blue & white. We're in the universe of lost things
where the lights are out,
the lamp pawned & soon the record player, that enameled table,
clothes, the rooms & faces,

air hissing soft through the rolled-down window like
silk velvet slipping hot
into my handbag, velvet fine as a fingerprint whorl,
maroon as the long dusty cars
that sharked these avenues, mildewed upholstery like
it was always raining night,
the insides ripped out of everything. But I was talking
about the red velvet jacket

that hangs even now in the mind flaring its slow veronicas
in recollection's wind that breathes
the mineral glamour of cornices & pilasters, districts
that burned years ago.
These days at the fringes even trains turn express,
the bombed-out blocks & clustered faces
blurred featureless. Out of sight, out of mind. Midnight's
burning highway, another charred strip-job.

Recollection: gather back the gleaming fragments & Warsaw flashes
a museum model of the Ghetto—
the Jews immured, a system of catwalks and barricades,
the trams' blackened windows

so that citizens might blindly pass, might invent consoling fictions.
Columns of flame light now
this tangled graffiti to a kind of incantation.
Called back in wonder,

the strangeness, the story endlessly told any life unfurls,
causal chains of small decisions,
almost random, those accidents of grace or luck. That red velvet
'30s jacket. How it sleeked
over the hips, elaborate glass buttons, how it made me feel
a little dangerous, a sense
of stolen fortune or history, as if I'd been chosen
for extraordinary moments, as if

I'd walk untouched, fire parting smoothly before me, liquid
& blue, that refused to singe,
to mar the bearer with a scar to signify the event.
Red velvet the color
of that long car we'd cruise under the river through Alphabetown,
then the Bronx, Hunts Point
& its flooded streets awash with crates of rotting fruit,
streets that figure still

relentless in the endless anarchy of dreams—
the Puerto Rican dealer, Juan, his wife, the kid. (Shift the car
to 5th, don't stop,
don't slow down.) But the door splinters all over again.
The jump-the-dealer routine.
Red velvet sleeve rolled up, snake of blue vein, snake
of salsa rising from the streets,
the warmth sexual, turning me capable, the grain of the wood

on the floor flowering into the music, each fiber,
each splinter, until the tree
it came from greened in the mind. No, it's the watery
green of neon flickering
the boy's face by the window, the baby in his arms dangling
over the street, the mother screaming.
His faced striped green & blue & the water of the neon
stutters turning Spanish

on my tongue. *Darme, darme el niño*. Accidental grace.
I just wanted the screaming to stop.
Someone muffles the mother, but he's watching me—sole white
    face,
blanched translucent—& across his face
all the complexity a gaze can be. Calculation at first, fear,
disdain, the crying child. And what
did he see? Some hopped-up 16-year-old with police-colored skin.

God I was innocent then, clean as a beast in the streets.
At the fringes of Warsaw's Ghetto
stands a prison where they sorted Jews from politicals,
politicals from homosexuals,
where masses dispersed to nameless erasure. There's a tree there,
lopped & blackened, yet it shines,
enshrined in prayer scrolls, nailed icons. Oh, lucky life,
I didn't understand until tonight,

called back from the ruins in that jacket, dark stain blooming
through the sleeve, the child squalling
in my useless arms. I don't know what happened to the jacket
& all those people are lost to a diaspora,

the borough incinerated around them, nowhere in this night
I drive through. Silk velvet and its rich hiss
the shade of flame offering its drapery, its charm
against this world burning ruthless, crucial & exacting.

Ornithology

Gone to seed, ailanthus, the poverty
   tree. Take a phrase, then
fracture it, the pods' gaudy nectarine shades
     ripening to parrots taking flight, all crest
and tail feathers.
              A musical idea.
                   Macaws

   scarlet and violet,
                  tangerine as a song
the hue of sunset where my street becomes water

and down shore this phantom city skyline's
   mere hazy silhouette. The alto's
liquid geometry weaves *a way of thinking,*
    a way of breaking
synchronistic
              through time
                    so the girl

    on the comer
              has the bones of my face,
the old photos, beneath the Kansas City hat,

black fedora lifting hair off my neck
   cooling the sweat of a night-long tidal
pull from bar to bar the night we went
    to find Bird's grave. Eric's chartreuse
perfume. That
             poured-on dress
                   I lived days

   and nights inside,

                    made love
and slept in, a mesh and slur of zipper

down the back. Women smoked the boulevards
    with gardenias after-hours, asphalt shower-
slick, ozone charging air with sixteenth
        notes, that endless convertible ride to find
the grave
                whose sleep and melody
                                    wept neglect
    enough to torch us
                        for a while
through snare-sweep of broom on pavement,

the rumpled musk of lover's sheets, charred
    cornices topping crosstown gutted buildings.
Torches us still—cat screech, matte blue steel
        of pistol stroked across the victim's cheek
where fleet shoes
                    jazz this dark
                                    and peeling
    block, that one.
                    Vine Street, Olive.
We had the music, but not the pyrotechnics—

rhinestone straps lashing my shoes, heels sinking
    through earth and Eric in casual drag,
mocha cheekbones rouged, that flawless
        plummy mouth. A style for moving,
heel tap and
                lighter flick,

                    lion moan
        of buses pulling away
                        through the static
brilliant fizz of taffeta on nyloned thighs.

Light mist, etherous, rinsed our faces
    and what happens when
you touch a finger to the cold stone
        that jazz and death played
down to?
            Phrases.
                Take it all
    and break forever—
                    a man
with gleaming sax, an open sill in summertime,

and the fire-escape's iron zigzag tumbles
    crazy notes to a girl cooling her knees,
wearing one of those dresses no one wears
        anymore, darts and spaghetti straps, glitzy
fabrics foaming
                an iron bedstead.
                            The horn's
    alarm, then fluid brass chromatics.
                            Extravagant
ailanthus, the courtyard's poverty tree is spike
and wing, slate-blue
                mourning dove,
                        sudden cardinal flame.

If you don't live it, it won't come out your horn.

Fiat Lux

Static from the radio stippled grey as anesthesia dream,
band after band of voices,
the luminous bar of speedometer, column shift. Cruising,
the long battered car fogged
in whiskey breath, the sumptuous trash, canvas scraps, pasteled
bills of lading. Father and daughter —

and over them blue spruce laden with snow arcing the white
mansioned avenue of robber barons'
palaces, the steamship magnates and celebrities, the city's
skyline gothamed electric
across the horizon. Small hands on the pane wick the chill
until I'm icy pure flame,

outside the big houses, streets unwinding below like a tulle scarf
from a woman's shoulders
to the damp wooden houses huddled in their steam, the marshes'
smoking blackness beyond. Swallow the moon like a coin,
an ivory poker chip polished

for luck, driving fast past the opera singer's house, his name
like nervous laughter, that
music blown to shards, arias of ice, and always the city's
dragon-back silhouette, someplace
a child might never get to. *Fiat lux*, the windows'
glow, buttery and old.

The city's become a figure for the way you've learned to love
what's distant, fantastic,
an abyss of space between. One of those returning things, skeins
of planetary days, lunar phases,

solar years turning harmonies celestial in the blood. One's
never done with the past.

Close your eyes. The laden winter night, hill tumbling down
and beneath the burning meadows'
spreading stain, the runaway's smoking train through roots, the blind
white worms and rat swarms
underneath the mercury-colored river. I always loved stories
that began that way: the elaborate entry

to the city of cast-iron garlands and window displays intricate
as a universe with shining cogs
and wheels, a world where night reversed to day, and towering
    women
waterfalled their Dynel tresses
in the shelter of marquees, boas spitting plumage in the faces
of nightwaiters.

Yes, the gilded birds, plunder in the turrets. And the pulse,
the mission, secret formulas
discovered all around me, the daughter swept in her black serge
dust-bin coat, tangled in foxtails,
glass eyes, shoplifter's pockets sewn inside stuffed with broken
    trinkets,
cancelled stamps from Peru and Mozambique.

Fingers tracing the skyline through the windshield of that battered
    car:
mere *fiat lux*, tricks,
delusions of sleek verb, the lustrous nouns. How to imagine
those places where chaos

holds sway, the old night where you hear scared laughter pierce
the anesthesia dream, song

of shoulders pushed rough to alley walls, torn caress, dark dress,
song that goes
I'll do it for 10, for 5, I'll do it, burnt spoon twisted in the pocket.
Don't tell her. Child stroking
the frosted pane, galactic, impervious and caught in this endless
coming to be that's endlessly undone,

the long car's weaving tracks blurred quickly in the snow beneath
the laden shelter of trees,
my father's whiskied breath as we drove like thieves through skeins
of planetary nights, air rich
with signals, the arias and perfect boundless schemes where
the city floated
distant and celestial, brutal in its own rung music.

Amulets

Riddled by seaworms, the figurehead's blind
unsurprised eyes gaze past a tattooed sailor's
hide, brindled with waves & fish, spreadeagled
on the wall, this coastal town museum. Clumsy
dioramas, ivory birdcages, the instruments of

celestial navigation. Down gallery,
in her battered leather jacket, I watch Emily
& her daughter kneel to spy through miniature
isinglass windows. An immense dollhouse:
each parlor, bedroom & hallway opening to

surprise, a mansion of possibility, each
salver & banister burnished to perfection.
The latest t-cell count report crumpled
in her pocket, she points to a tiny
muslin gown draping a chair as if just shrugged

from someone's shoulders freshly risen from
sleep's farthest shore, the shapes that flit
there—a man scarified with tidal waves
& floral demons, a harpy carved to plunge
like a diving horse from the ship's prow

through an ocean of ice. I need some amulet,
those charms we made as girls of locks
scissored from each other's hair
because mere faith did not seem harbor enough
in a world of brute possibility.

Or these pendants & bracelets woven entirely
of human hair. Storms of it—chestnut,
auburn, eternally growing, blue-sheened black,
ashen blond pulled from brushes, combs, soaked
& dried, combed & knotted, shellacked

with yellow sealing wax. Talismans.
The ill-typed card of explanation warps
through the glass case, currents & bubbles
rippling the whirr of voices diminuendoed
when I close my eyes to watch, like vision,

half-remembered, pulled from dream,
black mares beneath their plumes dragging
a cortège, crepe-hung, through heavy pearled
sands, a stinging hiss of ocean swallowing
one more name, some pestilence, women

letting down storms of wavy hair, though it's only
a sepiaed photo I'm recalling, Grandmother
& her sisters with their jewel names,
Opal, Ruby, Sapphire, posed in a parlor
for tableaux vivants—the Graces

with their billowing knee-length tresses, loose
white gowns, but I should have thought of them
as Fates, the trio set afloat beyond
the farthest shores lofting pearl-handled scissors
against whole skeins of thread. Gale-force winds

rattle locks, breathe ragged around the walls
like black horses laboring through sand, fears
given form, phantoms a child might magically
appease. We did it all wrong. Emily, who says
she's never felt looked over, never been

protected, or spared. What I hear is
her laughter, the child's long aspirant *ahhh*
of wonder. What I need is some talisman, an amulet,
the old cosmology with its crystalline
perfection of shells around the world, celestial

frictive music to navigate by. Who'd want
to surrender? Skies pearled cold, the sea's
lullaby crooned in the shell of the ear,
I know, the houses scrawled by moonlight
down the hill, salted around the bay frozen

to filigree, smooth floes of ice. Nervous
hands twisting, Emily braids her long hair,
rich as a mare's tail cascading, scars
mapping each vein with the addict's tattoo:
her immune system's failing.

How do I place them standing like figures
in a glass case, shore's edge where sand pearls
beneath the dome of stars—a world
safe & comprehensible? How is a spell woven,
like these jewels, through the hours' twilit progress?

Braids ovalling silhouettes meant for wearing
like holy medals against bare skin. Starbursts,
whorls inspiraled as the heart of a nebula,
charms meant to cheat fate, to stay the journeyer
a little while longer, who'll never pass this way again.

River Bridge

Winter, stepping into the night trolley,
quarter pint of scotch in pocket. . . *No not that one.*
The childhood story—Grandmother reading among
her violets a poem about the elevated train
slithering its worm down London's spine.
Not that one. I could tell you skeins
of train stories, as now through this dense
summer night, trees swarming green their canopy
over the street of warm lit windows, the train
slashes its path through the neighborhood, whirr
and pulse, the heart and fuse of distance filling
the room, hurtling through countless frames,
the scenes—now that curtainless room of young men
preening shirtless before their mirrors, now
the ward of iron hospital beds. *I've seen them.*
By the screen, the white cat swivels her ears
to follow the train until it's lost in glass
smashing, the alley voices. Who's walking tonight?
Who's hungry? The story I keep returning to
is the one about walking hungry over
that St. Louis railroad bridge. *Why that one?*
Is it the bridge? Bridge linking one riverbank aflame
in smokestacks, the slaughterhouses, to
the bank where the city's glittering Andromeda
spilled itself before them. Bridge
of flying hands and curses, iron bridge
and the passage of colliers, boxcars, the gondolas
freighting coal, dull sprockets,
sleek carriages of lingerie and crystal.

Distant, the sceptered city glints, a figment,
I could begin. Or *once, there was a time,*
the opening a fairy tale, simple, sinister.

II

January, its savage tempers & mirthless
North wind have iced the iron bridge's spans.
Between flaming riverbanks, the two walk thin
as flame, a world refined to fierce purity—
lungs blued to filigree, bare ankle, damp sleeve
frosted beneath the other's steadying hand.
Stepping tie to tie,
the river churned below
its suicide babble, the nitrous drowned
sopranos, sulfuric moans. Such a grand manner
of entry, fareless, in stealth,
the city's lit gateway fuming like midnight's
wild schemes. Should I ask the obvious questions?
Such as what was the engine driving the machine
of their travel? Oh, fear, that's familiar. Folly,
leavened recklessly with hope. Lights multiply
against the sky, the city's slow Andromeda,
a constellation the shape of what they seek,
the streets *inside* of Berlined façades, people
breakfasting in mid-air, walls torn down. The squatter's
palace. The rat's domain, each moment rinsed
in benzine, sharpened with amphetamine,
the hunger. Alluvial voices
hissing beneath them *dogs of chaos,*
escape from the burning city, no time, no time.

The river knows the story. The get-out of-town-fast story.
A dizzy trip through the ripped underside of things —
that rough fugitive coinage, begged rides,
begged meals. Somebody fed us. Somebody said
get out of town. Those E. St. Louis backyards sooty
with frozen laundry trees. Should I say the Mississippi knows
the story of the room left behind, the bad deals?
Like a scene playing out in a glass globe
I might hold in my palm, I can watch them:
oh look at those fools, the cold carving
them up to some version of bewildered miracle.

        III

Deep freeze humming the rails, the entrance
into the unknown city, the bus station pulsing
fluorescent waves across ranks of pay TVs,
a quarter a view for those laying over, for those
mired in dim rooms, too long alone with themselves.
You know how it is. The fact of death starts pearling
large in the mind, darkening its banks of offices,
ballrooms where you might touch some face
you recognize, those staircases that spiral, collapse
amidst the body's mysteries, its harsh betrayals.
Or love's betrayals. Through static, the P.A. spits
destinations, frayed galaxies of names — *Columbus,
Joplin, St. Joe, Points West, Kansas City. . . .*
How does one thing part from another? Redrawing tendrils
& roots, a lopped amputation that leaves this one
raving in the street, the other cold, cold . . .
alone in the room after such intensity, the way

it would be, me leaving E. so crassly after
the crazy journey. I think now I've become
a character in this, must slip on the coat,
these salt-wet shoes, sip the raw whiskey
and in the drunken radiance the TVs spill
over sleepers' faces hear the late-night tapdancers,
the anthems & jets. Then the station signal's
high bat-cry peeling away to the automated
voice, *Chicago, Detroit, Points North.* . . .
After the parting, one from the other, there's
the long reclamation, flood plain, phantom
limb. From one form to another: transit.

    IV

Oh, the anarchy of owning nothing
but a constellation the shape of what they seek.
The get-out-of-town-fast story. No bus fare,
and where to go
in this steaming plenty, the lit kitchens
& parlors glimpsed from the street washed
citron by lamplight. Is it the stolen car
again in this version, or the abandoned movie palace?
I can put them in the theater and show them
making love, warm with each other
& the begged bottle of scotch & they can sleep
in moldering velvets. Stripped bare,
sapphired in blue air, she'd be a woman served
to the city's glittering Andromeda.
Like the Russian cellist broke in Berlin,
the '20s, who'd sleep in the opera house, who

one delirious night played, naked, his instrument
into the shadows, the banked silent seats
& rat galleries. And forgot the cold.
That would be pretty wouldn't it?
But the theater's barricaded, and so,
it must be, as it always is, the stolen car.
Beyond the city it will spirit them
into the blizzard, the etherous drifts, until
the engine stops & the road erases, trackless.
And then she'll know ice needling the blood
to scarlet foliage. But, how to show the calm
when she thinks, *so this is what it's like to die*,
a twisting bolt of black cloth dragged back
through stations, the bare dusty rooms, chalk dust
& sachet, the river's voices
deep nitrous green. How calm. Pocking snow
on the windshield, heavy and damp as the voices
of crows in her grandmother's trees,
a cry she mimicked at the back of her throat,
harsh and wild. White crows
now blessing her eyes. How calm.

V

When the authorities lifted them away
from there, they entered a world of steam,
that fallen roadside constellation chromed
with coffee urns, galaxies of white plates.
Crossing the bridge back, again, the blood's
fierce arterial surge like arias, like
alarming camellias scarlet with snow

still frosting the ground. Heavy and warm,
cups of coffee steamed in our hands, the good
bitter coffee. But always, we were aware,
hear still, the pulse and singing:
I am the stranger coiled on the landing, singing
this is the bridge of the flying hands,
the mansion of the body. I am the one
who scratched at your door, the one who begged
rough coinage. This is the blessing
& this a hymnal of wings. Hear the heart's
greedy alluvial choir, a cascading train
whirring the tracks: called back,
called back from the river.

VI

Chirring in her throat the white cat stretches
on the sill, all ruffled ivory, present-tense,
muscular pure. Can one possess a clear vision
of oneself in the world? Dominion over
all that bewildering wrack? This raised hand
against the evening's towering cream and smoke
conjures a flurry of ghost hands, a crowd
glimpsed blurred from the hurtling train. Clouds
billow & unknot a sudden shower releasing
that lavish wet asphalt perfume, the fragrance
of countless showers over scores of cities, each one
intensely *now, now, this sweet wrenched only.*
From the turbulent river, moments swim unbidden
to the surface, others never rise at all, the lost
drowned arias, sunken avenues of camphored rooms,

the walls with their watery initials. Phantom
destinations, the P.A.'s *St. Joe, Kansas City,
Denver*, points beyond the laden plains surging
beneath waves of snow, blue perilous mountains,
locales in the mind.
The cat leaps, again a train, striking this time
a smooth oiled chord, as if there might be
singing on the other side of the tracks.
Some Jordan. That otherness, those secret times,
the bridges beneath the surface of a life.
Pull on the rough coat and salt-wet shoes.
Let the liquor burn your throat. Did I do that?
Could that have been me? Those figures crossing
the bridge, setting out, always setting out.
Voices I must keep listening for in these sharpening
leaves, among the stacks and flames,
the smoking pillars. *Someone fed them.*
Someone said get out of town.

TWO

Suite for Emily

1. The Letter

Everywhere the windows give up nothing
but frost's intricate veined foliage.
Just engines shrilling pocked and frozen streets
wailing toward some new disaster.
No *bright* angels' ladders going to split
heaven this Chicago instant where the pier's
an iced fantastic: spiked, the glacial floes
seize it greedy like a careless treasure —

marquise diamonds, these round clear globes, the psychic's
crystal world spinning in her corner shop
when I passed, a globe boundaried with turning
silent winds and demons. Out here the pavement's
a slick graffitied strip: *There's more to life*
than violence. Someone's added *Yes, Sex and Drugs.*
Hello, Plague Angel. I just heard your wings
hiss off the letter on my table — Emily's

in prison again, her child's lost to the State,
Massachusetts. Fatigue, pneumonia,
the wasting away. In the secret hungering,
the emptiness when we were young would come
the drug's good sweep like nothing else,
godly almost the way we'd float immune
& couldn't nothing touch us, nothing.
Somehow I'd thought you'd pass her over —

positive yes — but never really sick,
that flayed above her door there'd be some sign

of mercy. But there's only January's
rough ministry peeling my face away.
Light like the cruel light of another century
& I'm thinking of Dickinson's letter,
"Many who were in their bloom have gone
to their last account and the mourners go about

the streets." The primer pages yellowing
on her shelf beneath an album of pressed gentian:
"Do most people live to be old? No, one half die
before they are eight years old. But one in four lives
to see twenty-one." She'd known the bitter sponge
pressed to the fevered forehead, the Death Angel's
dark familiar company, how she'd swirl her veils,
how she'd lean over the ewer and basin

blackening the water. This arctic water, this
seething rustle—lamé, sequins, a glitter wrap
trailing from a girl's shoulders so the shadow pimps
go *hey princess, why you so sad tonight,*
let me make you happy, when she's only tired,
up all night & needing a hit to let her sleep.
We know that story, the crest and billow
& foam and fleeting fullness

before the disappearing. Discs of hissing ice,
doors you (I?) might fall through to the underworld
of bars & bus stations, private rooms of
dancing girls numb-sick & cursing the wilderness
of men's round blank faces. Spinning demons.
Round spoon of powder hissing over the flame.

Worlds within worlds, beneath worlds, worlds that flare
and consume so they become the only world.

   2. Holy City, City of Night

What is that general rule which tells
   how long a thing will live? The primer answers,
Whatever grows quick decays quick: soon ripe,
   soon rotten. The rust-blown calla gracing
my table, those Boston girls 20 years gone,
young men in lace & glitter washed alien
   by gasoline sunsets, the burning sphere
lapsing below night's black rim. *Live fast, die. . .*

we know the rest. Reckless anthem.
   The pier cable's ice-sleeved beneath
my hands—miraculous, yes, to be here
   januaried by this lake's barbaric winterscape
Dickinson might read as savage text
& emblem of a deity indifferent. Her embassy lay
   beyond the city of jasper & gold, the beaten
wrought towers scripture promised the saved

would enter. What heaven she found she made.
   And so did we, worlds that sear, consume—earthly,
delirious. *Ignis fatuus.* Strike the match,
   the fizzing cap. But Oh Reader, the wild beauty
of it, the whirring rush, blond hiss of aerial
miles, worn stairways in every burning school
   of nodding classrooms, the buzz-snap of
talk blurring hallucinatory fraught

avenues. Illusive inner city, drugged
    majestic residence spiraled with staircases,
balustrades rococoed, lapidary. Invisible empires
    dreamt beneath the witchery of birds
circling the Common with twilight, their caw
& settle, the patterns as they wheel
    over the pond's reflective mirror bruised
roseate, violet, deeper, the swanboats

darkening into night's charged dazzle,
    Park Square joints gone radiant, the bus station
burnished before the zap, the charge, the edge.
    It was the life wasn't it? Compatriots you'd
just love to die for, who'd jump you
in a New York minute. But the glory
    as the lights went up, torching the air chartreuse,
lipsticked pink, casting embers, seraphic fires

fallen earthward. Fallen, the furious emblems.
    We were so young we'd spend & spend
ourselves as if there'd be no reckoning, then grew
    past caring. All the darkening chapters.
Dream time, the inner time
where towers and battlements erect
    their coruscating glamour & how we'd glide,
celebrities among them, the crowds falling back,

dream deeper, gone & wake to daylight's assault
    knocking another bare room, the alley, the bathroom
you inhabit like the thief you are. *Ignis fatuus*.
    I can follow you there, Emily, we girls

setting out a thousand ruined nights in the splendor
of the torched & reckless hour.
   Who wouldn't trade heaven for that fleet city
when winter beaks the shattered pane,

when summer's a nauseous shimmer
   of sexual heat, though sex is a numb machine
you float above? When the place you walk into
   is a scream in the shape of yourself.
When it makes perfect sense to blow someone away
for 20 bucks beyond even your bleak human universe.
   When the only laughter that falls down
is iron & godless. Here, I—the one who left—

must falter where persists
   this chrome traffic shrill, where the cable's
bitter alloy comes away in my hand,
   this metaled pungence of hair and skin
in wind persists riven as the taste of myself,
the blood blooming healthy,
   real in my mouth, a future's lavish venues
spread stunned before me. These hands.

   3. Combat Zone/War Stories

The district's been demolished, sown with salt.
The dazzling girls, girls, girls in platinum wigs
have been lifted away by some infernal agency,
the queens, exotic Amazons & rough-trade gay boys.

Sometimes I go back to walk the streets all shops
and swank hotels, the office blocks & occasional
burnt-out shell. So American, this destruction
& renewal, cities amnesiac where evening's

genesis falls through vast deserted silences,
towers grown otherworldly with light
thrown starlike from some alien world. Gone the Show Bar,
the Mousetrap, the whole gaudy necklace

of lacquer-dark underground lounges, halls
of mirrors, music billowing dancers
clean out of themselves beyond the dead-faced tricks,
the sick voyeurs. The Combat Zone. I can map it

in my mind, some parallel world, the ghost city
beneath the city. Parallel lives, the ones
I didn't choose, the one that kept her.
In all that dangerous cobalt luster

where was safety? Home? When we were delirium
on rooftops, the sudden thrill of wind dervishing
cellophane, the shredded cigarettes. We were
the dust the Haitians spit on to commemorate

the dead, the click & slurried fall of beads
across a doorway. In the torn & watered silk
of night, the Zone exploded its shoddy neon orchid
to swallow us in the scent of fear, emergency,

that oily street perfume & weeping brick.
Gossamer clothes, summertime and leaning
against the long dusty cars, cruising siren songs.
Summer? My memory flutters — had I — was there summer?

Dancer, and floor, and cadence
quite gathered away, and I a phantom, to you
a phantom, rehearse the story.
And now it's autumn turning hard to winter,

Thanksgiving, 1990, & all she wants is sweets
so it's apple pie barehanded & Emily's
spinning war stories, how bad she is: *So, I say,*
go ahead and shoot me, put me out of my misery.

Cut me motherfucker — my blood's gonna kill you.
Then she's too tired to sit & in the blue
kaleidoscopic TV shift I stroke
her hair, the ruined hands. *I didn't know*

how sick I was — if the heroin wanted the AIDS,
or if the disease wanted the heroin. She asks me
to line up her collection of matchbox houses
so we can make a street, so we can make a neighborhood.

   4. Jail, Flames — Jersey, 1971

The psychic's globe whirls its winds: demons,
   countless futures, the pasts. Only
      thirteen the first time

I saw you in jail, just a kid looking
up at me, the usual grey detective clamor,

inkpads & sodium flash. Hauled out by the officials,
    exemplary bad-news girl, they shoved
        a lyric sheet at me. Command
    recitation to sway you from straying.
"King Heroin," James Brown pompadoured like nobody's

business & here's Death cartoonishly aloft on a white
    winged horse, grim reaper lording it
        over the shivering denizens
    of a city, exaggerated as any Holy City,
going down, down, down. Just a kid, you, peering out

the jungle of your dark hair, greasy jeans, a tangle
    of beads at your throat. Ludicrous,
        I know, me declaiming within
    the jail gleam that never sleeps all over us,
that effluvium of backed-up plumbing. On my palm,

the bar's iron taint lingered for hours after.
    It didn't mean that much to me, seventeen,
        my practiced sangfroid
    chilling the terror, that long drop
inside, the way you collapse to fall in flames.

I might have said you'll pay for the wild & reckless hour,
    pay in the currency of sweat and shiver,
        the future squandered, the course

of years reconfigured, relinquishment so
complete it's more utter than any falling in love. Falling

instead in flames, burning tiles spiraling to litter
   the courtyards of countless places that will
      never be yours, the fingerprints,
   tossed gloves & glittering costumes, flared
cornices & parapets, shattering panes, smoked out

or streaked with embers, the tinder of spools, such
   a savage conflagration, stupid edge-game,
      the way junkies tempt death,
   over & over again, toy with it. I might have
told you that. Everything you ever meant to be, *pfft*,

out the window in sulphured matchlight, slow tinder
   & strike, possession purely ardent as worship
      & the scream working its way out
   of your bones, demolition of wall & strut
within until you're stark animal need. That *is*

love, isn't it? Everything you meant to be falls
   away so you dwell within a perfect
      singularity, a kind of saint.
   Pearl of great price. Majestic, searing,
the crystal globe spins futures unimaginable, that

crucible you know so well, Emily, viral fever refining
   you to some essence of pain more furious
      than these winter trees

stripped to black nerves above
the El's streaked girders, a harsh equation, some

god's iron laughter combing down time's blind
    & hush. *Hush child, forgive me.*
      Twenty years later, you say
    that night in jail you looked up
at me & wanted to be me. And I didn't care.

   5. Address

Hello Death Angel, old familiar, old nemesis.
    In the deepest hours, I have recognized
your floating shape. I've seen your breath
    seduce the torn curtain
masking the empty window, have crouched with you
    in the doorway, curled in the alley
hooded in your essence & shadow, have
    been left blue, heart-stopped
for yours, for yours. Death,
    you are the bead in the raptor's eye,
Death you dwell in the funneling depths
    of the heavens beyond each
star's keening shrill, Death you are the potion
    that fills the vial, the night
the monuments have swallowed. You live
    in the maimed child wrapped in a wreckage
of headlines. Death you center
    in the fanged oval
of the prison dog's howl. Death you dwell within
    the necropolis we wake to in nightmare's

hot electric wind. You glint
    the edge of the boy's razor,
patient in the blasted stairwell. Everywhere
    you walk deep lawns, TVs pollinating air
with animals wired up to dance
    for their food, with executions
& quiz shows. You're in the column
    of subway wind roaring before each
train's arrival. I've seen you drape thoughtlessly
    a woman's hair over her face
as the shot carried her forward into stop-time
    & beyond anything she'd laid
her money down for. Death your sliver works
    swiftly through the bloodstream.
Hello Death Angel, Plague is your sister.
    I've seen her handiwork, heard
the tortured breath, watched her loosen the hands
    of the dazzling boys one from each other.
For love, love. I've seen the AIDS hotels
    & sick ones begging homeless
in the tunnels, the whispered conspiracies.
    Shameless emissaries with your powders
& wands, your lunar carnivorous flowers.
    Tricks, legerdemain. I've seen you draw
veined wings over the faces of sleepers,
    the abandoned, the black feather that sweeps
so tenderly. I've seen the stain you scribe
    on the pavement, the glossy canopy of leaves
you weave. I've seen waste & ruin, know
    your kingdom for delirium, the furious thumbprints
you've scored on the flesh of those you choose.

I've seen you slow-dance in a velvet mask, dip
& swirl across dissolving parquet.
    I've seen you swing open the iron gate —
a garden spired in valerian, skullcap, blue vervain.
    Seen you stir the neat half-moons, fingernails
left absently in a glazed dish.
    Felons, I've cursed you in your greed, have spat
& wept then acquiesced in your wake. Without rue
    or pity, you have marked the lintels & blackened
the water. Your guises multiply, bewildering
    as the firmament's careless jewelry.
Death I have welcomed you to the rooms
    where Plague has lain when the struggle is passed
& lit the candles and blessed the ash.
    Death you have taken my friends & dwell
with my friends. You are the human wage.
    Death I am tired of you.

6. Dartmouth Women's Prison, 1992

Emily, delirium's your province.
You dwell feverish in prison
voiceless to plead
your need before the agencies
of government who *cannot hear the buildings*
falling & oil exploding, only people walking
& talking, cannon soft as velvet from parishes
that do not know you are burning up,
that seasons have rippled
like a beast the grasses beyond
the prison.

They cannot hear the strummed harp
or the nerves, black trees swaying winter,
cannot know your child is lost to you.

The human wage that's paid & paid?

Once, we were two girls
setting out toward that city
of endless searing night, the route taking on
the intricacy, the fumes & bafflements
of a life a woman might dream turning
feverish in her prison bunk. Probation violation,
when broke & sick, no way home
from the clinic, the detective going
ride with me, just talk, that's all
I want. Twenty bucks and him crowing
we just love to run you little sluts in.

Em, if I could reach you through the dust motes'
spinning, infernoed dreams, I would dwell
in the moon's cool glistering
your cell, the rough cloth, the reflection
of your face given back in the steel basin's
water, in the smooth moan of women loving women,
a cacophony of needs. I am there with you lost
in the chaos of numbers, that nattering P.A. buzz,
in the guards' trolling clank & threat echoing
walls so eloquent
with all the high-frequency sizzle
of anguish they've absorbed.
Emily, I will bless your child, will

hold for you the bitter sponge,
would give you staff & orb, a firmament
radiant & free.

But these are phantoms, lies—
I cannot follow where you are. On my street,
the psychic's crystal globe whirls pasts, futures
but where you are is timeless.
Pain—has an Element of Blank—It cannot recollect
when it Began—or if there were
a time when it was not—
It has no Future—but itself . . .

Off the lake a toothed wind keens
& it's just me here, the one who's left.
Just me helpless to change anything caught
in this ellipsis between traffic, this
fleet human delay, all around
the wind singing like a mechanical ballerina
a girl might hold in her hand, the one
that watched your childhood bed, porcelain
upturned gaze, stiff tutu, dust in the folds
of that spindly piercing music sounding
of voices winged over water, becoming
water, & gone.

7. A Style of Prayer

There is a prayer that goes Lord I am powerless
  over these carnivorous streets, the fabulous
    breakage, the world's ceaseless *perpetuum mobile,*

like some renaissance design, lovely & useless
   to harness the forces of weather, the planet's
      dizzy spin, this plague. A prayer that asks

where in the hour's dark moil is mercy?
   Ain't no ladders tumbling down from heaven
      for what heaven we had we made. An embassy

of ashes & dust. Where was safety? Home?
   Is this love, staff, orb & firmament?
      Parallel worlds, worlds within worlds—chutes

& trapdoors in the mind. Sisters & brothers,
   the same thing's going down all over town, town
      after town. There is a prayer that goes Lord,

we are responsible. Harrow us through the waves,
   the runnels & lace that pound, comb, reduce us so
      we may be vessels for these stories.

Oh, the dazzling men torn one from the other,
   these women taken, these motherless children.
      Perhaps there's no one to fashion such new grace,

the world hurtling its blind proposition
   through space & prayer's merely a style of waiting
      beyond *the Hour of Lead*—

Remembered, if outlived,
   As Freezing persons, recollect the Snow—
      First Chill—then Stupor—then the letting go . . .

But oh, let Emily become anything
    but the harp she is, too human, to shiver
        grievous such wracked & torn discord. Let her be

the foam driven before the wind over the lakes,
    over the seas, the powdery glow floating
        the street with evening—saffron, rose, sienna

bricks, matte gold, to be the good steam
    clanking pipes, that warm music glazing the panes,
        each fugitive moment the heaven we choose to make.

~ THREE

Rivers into Seas

Palaces of drift and crystal, the clouds
loosen their burden, unworldly flakes so thick
the border zones of sea and shore, the boundless zones
of air fuse to float their worlds until the spirits
congregate, fleet histories yearning into shape.

Close my eyes and I'm a vessel. Make it
some lucent amphora, Venetian blue, lip circled
in faded gold. Can you see the whorls of breath,
imperfections, the navel where it was blown
from the maker's pipe, can you see it drawn

up from the bay where flakes hiss the instant
they become the bay? Part the curtain. The foghorn's
steady, soothing moan—warning, safety, the reeling
home. Shipwreck and rescue. Stories within stories—
there's this one of the cottage nestled into dune

snowed into pure wave, the bay beyond and its lavish
rustle, skirts lifting and falling fringed in foam.
But I'm in another season—my friends' house adrift,
Wally's last spring-into-summer, his bed a raft,
cats and dogs clustered and we're watching television

floods, the Mississippi drowning whole cities
unfamiliar. How could any form be a vessel
adequate to such becoming, the stories unspooled
through the skein of months as the virus erased
more and more until Wally's nimbused as these

storm clouds, the sudden glowing ladders they let fall?
But that's not the moment I'm conjuring—it's when
my voyager afloat so many months brought back
every flood story I carried. Drifting worlds,
and Wai Min takes a shape I tell Wally as

steady watermarks across the cold bare floor—
Chinatown, South Pacific flashing its crimson,
neoned waves tranced across Wai Min's midnight eyes
behind black shades, and that voice unraveling past
each knocking winter pane. It's another world

I'm telling. Cognac and squalor. The foghorn's haunting drone
blends with that halting monotone, scarlet watermarks,
the Sinkiang's floodtides murky brown, the village
become water, swept away. Three days floating on a door,
his sister, the grandmother weaving stories endless

beneath the waxed umbrella canopy she's fashioned,
stories to soothe the children wrapped in the curtain
of her hair, to calm the ghost souls' blurred lanterns.
How rats swam to their raft, soaked cats, spirits
she said, ghosts held tranced by the storied murmurous

river. I have no spell, simply the foghorn's song
when voices unbodied, drift over water past
the low dune this cottage nestles in becoming
shape in motion stilled. No boundaries on this point,
foghorn singing its come-home incantation over

the ruthless currents. And isn't it so
we're merely vessels given in grace, in mystery,
just a little while, our fleet streaked moments?
As this day is given, singular, chilly
bolts of snow chenilled across the sky, the sea.

How to cipher where one life begins and becomes
another? Part the curtain and here's my voyager
afloat, gentle sleeper, sweet fish, dancer over
water and he's talking, laughing in
that great four-poster bed he could not leave

for months, a raft to buoy his furious radiant soul,
if I may so hazard to say that? Yes,
there was laughter, the stories, the shining dogs—
gold and black—his company. Voyager afloat
so many months, banks of sunflowers he loved spitting

their seeds. Tick. Black numerals on the sill.
A world can be built anywhere & he spun, letting go. . . .
The last time I held him, the last time we spoke, just
a whisper—hoarse—that marries now this many-voiced mansion
of storm and from him I've learned to slip my body,

to be the storm governed by the law of bounty given
then taken away. Shush and glide. This tide's running
high, its silken muscular tearing ruled by cycles,
relentless, the drawn lavish damasks—teal, aquamarine,
silvered steel, desire's tidal forces, such urgent

fullness, the elaborate collapse, and withdrawal
beyond the drawn curtain that shows the secret
desert of bare ruched sand. I've learned this,
I've learned to be the horn calling home
the journeyer, saying farewell. And here's

the foghorn's simple two-note wail,
mechanical stark aria that ripples
out to shelter all of us—
our mortal burden of dreams—
adrift in the sea's restless shouldering.

For Wally Roberts, 1951–1994

Street of Crocodiles

April's chill glistens this prospect
of tarpaper roofs spreading their planes,
steam hammering pipes, mist ghosting
warming earth. In rivulets, rain casts

patterns, kaleidoscopic across windowsill
charms & artifacts. This doll,
this doll maddening with the secrecy of
her celluloid trance, rotting spirals of veil

binding her head, its trepanned crown, the disc
of skull the toymaker reached through to trigger
the lead mechanism that works her eyes. Reaches
now through the ruins, his swift gesture

seven decades gone, hands erased with the doll world
jittering its silent movies, & kinetoscopes,
maps to places that no longer exist, old empires.
Tilted, she's suddenly blind, mouth opened

as if to speak, to cry out. Hairless,
her body's evaporated to air.
The lead weight that rolls her glass eyes
hangs naked below the neck. Turn her around.

A Star of David spikes its points between
the dollmaker's initials. Below that
an oval circling *Polska*. Tilt again
and her lidless eyes resume their gaze. Lashes

& brows handpainted, exquisite, cheeks tinted
to the blush a girl might have on a chill day
gathering mushrooms. *Drive to the Vistula,*
my mother said, *the old square.* We're geomancing

for remnants. Our lost cousins found returning
with mushrooms, basketsful to wash, to hang
on strands of twine webbing their kitchen.
A lineage freighted & intricate as

these fissures across the doll's forehead,
her cheek. Irises spoked the peerless blue
of delphinium petals fallen to pale
in their dying. What fills that empty head?

Unblinking eyes that know the story?
How some made steerage & grew sleek, & the many
were left to be divided, to be dealt
the yellow cards of the murdered, to know

childhood's airless breathing spiderwebs,
the must of between-the-secret-convent-walls.
To know the stopped throat of the hidden. And so
we arrived with the sheen of the spared,

& they gathered & there was much weeping,
the language unspoken for decades winging
awkward in my mother's throat. *Blood of our blood.*
Polish, shushes and wings my throat with *zimna,*

boli, glodny, rodzina. Word for cold, for pain,
the word for hunger, & for family. Lead weight
hangs in the neck, stopping the throat.
When I came home from Poland . . . I could not speak.

    ˌ ˌ ˌ

Ceaseless oiled glide of trains
through the tops of trees & wail of the express:
song of *we don't stop here.* But we must
linger with Stacia who gazes through my mother's

face, my own, through the knee-length drapery
of her hair. Let's begin again.
With this celluloid doll, severed head, let
her sing Orphean of her breakage, of history's

ageless demons, leather-winged swarms, colonnades
& epic monuments they contrive—Krakow's
burning cathedral whose air thickens with incense,
with whispered sins, conspiracies. Or the Kingdom

of Auschwitz with its mountains, the shorn hair
of 40,000 women turned gray by Zyklon B,
the piled canisters & shoes, galleries
of photographs lining the walls, mute testaments

to the eloquent & terrible erasures.
The scrap of cloth, the violin case, this doll, stained
by the oils of human hands, worn by the skin.
If I hold this doll, if I drop to my knees

will something of the soul inhere? Brief
electric joys, mordant taint of fear,
something of the prayers & curses.
Empty head, all my life I've slept through dreams

that weren't my own & now we arrive again
at the place you were afraid of—the hem
of the mannequin's dress on its iron rim lufting
soft the spring air, another April, dark wine rose

among the flounces, the dress form poised
for fitting, the soup bowls left steaming
when my uncles were taken. When the children
returned, the flat mid-air, building bombed

& fragile, the bowls waited, the winds half-
forgetful lifting the rotten lace on the dress
made for a sister who would never wear it,
who left the world naked, bald. Tilt the doll,

make her blind again, the time
                                        of childhood is past & over.

        ⸱⸰ ⸱⸰ ⸱⸰

Though nothing's past & over. This doll's hollow skull
bears the dollmaker's touch turned to dust.
Lead weight gagging the throat & oh, to grow mute
as this celluloid head. The stuff of stiff collars,

of newsreels. Let the houselights dim, the projector's
shivering beam & we enter the *Street of Crocodiles*,

where twin filmmakers—the Brothers Quay—make
us fall through a kinetoscope to a warren

of streets, begrimed, webbed with a system
of terrible machines. Dolls with blind & numbered
heads perform their monstrous surgeries through
the murmurous river of narration, the voice

Polish, soft & dark. We are meant to think
of Mengele, of the shuddering names.
Auschwitz, Birkenau where day and night sky
flamed vermilion and ash. A child said it was like

a movie—watching over & over the transports arrive.
Mengele waiting, the Death Angel elegant
with his white gloved hand tilting right, left,
labor or crematorium. He let the twins

keep their hair, garbed them in sailor suits,
silk dresses. Once he knelt down
and whispered to a girl, *your mother
is in that chimney, your family.*

Maybe I'll call this doll Clio after
the cruelest Muse, blank History, her pages
waiting to fill. Her mouth's perfect bow
parts—as if to cry out, as if surprised, aggrieved

at this world where Destiny, where God
has grown famous because they answer us with silence.

Her silence swarms packed as the dust motes
in Poland, how we walked among whispers shriven

from air, lingering remnants, the unbodied shards:
a river tossed by whitecaps before the freshening
spring. A sky foaming jade, cobalt. Yellow fabric
of a dress run through the hands, the full sweet taste

of cream. Pages waiting for their ink, for
everything damned, for everything human & lovely.

Denouement

In the house, the emptied rooms, sand hushing
across bare floors, the open trunks and suitcases.

Dissolving shore, church spire and lighthouse,
we are always ready to leave, expert only

in departures, and I'm impresario
of the moment, the sky's peerless imperial

blue, combers foaming to glassy ripples
intricate as the mind, taking this all in.

Good-bye to young men strolling arm in arm,
isolate silhouettes of women glimpsed

through gauzy scarves billowing sheer
seductive semaphores. Wind off the open sea

whips the bay's wavelets to rush before it
all cresting spray. Think foaming manes

of little white mares in flight, lace froth
of a dancer's skirt lifting in the zephyr of

her arabesque gone acru into dust,
the pages of a book fanning to a whisper

tossed table to table. Berlin in 1927,
the Allaverdi's cellar club for exiles.

Now silence when the men bow toward
a shawl-draped woman who stands then sheds

her wrap. Pavlova, her career near its end.
Still she whispers to the violinist

and the crowd fades back, the drawn bow, en pointe
she sways. It could be easy now to pause,

remark the century's lunatic choreography,
or shall I go on? The drawn bow as en pointe

she sways, it's true, the final moment
of The Dying Swan. I could show her

floating, a phantom into that narrow space . . .
No, only sea breeze, these open trunks,

sand buffing the floor. I must shape elaborate
historical parallels, but her supple arms—

at hand in this spindrift instant—fishermen's
grievous bells over water, young men preening

mirrored in the shopwindows. It's simply
spring wind sculpting the bay to the lace

of a dancer's skirt and once more
I'm leaving and, just now, thought of Pavlova.

How beneath the vaulted ceiling her body sank
to the stone floor, and so like a swan's, her neck

curved smooth when the cheering crowd arose
with shadow cupped in palms before applause.

For Ann

1936–1991

The years have verdigrised the fallen leaves
on the pilgrim's monument you loved — horses'
arched necks straining toward autumn, summer's
last sultry declension. The night of the call
was the night of the planets, of gauzy cirrus
whipped, fiery seraphim cruising an atmosphere
of whispered conversations, soft alto laughter

wreathed in smoky helixes, smoke that fogged
Ann's face as she'd lean forward, a cup
held, girlish, in both hands. The night
I learned of her death, we walked
and found again that single child's ballet
slipper at shoreline. Boundaries. Water
and singing stones, day world to night world,

seasons turning one to the other, bay to open ocean.
That was the night the lacquered monkeys wove
their paws through a woman's plaited hair —
the psychic's display, and her crystal globe
of the world marked with its boundaries, winds
and demons turning silently in the window.
On that globe this night must show, the night

of the girl on the rocks tossing garlands
of freesia and dahlias, earrings into the water,
the waves' incantation, over and over, runnel
to ascent and crest, the torn lace of collapse.
The singing stones, the night the bandaged ward

shut down, morphine swaddles her riddled body.
The night somewhere, the first time, a child kickturns

in its amniotic sea, and a girl walks trailing
from her shoulders a glitter wrap so
the shadow pimps go *hey princess,*
why you so sad tonight. Freesias and dahlias
on the water, violet, rippling like a beast
in the breeze, dahlias straggling
the streets of that wooden town by the sea

where I knew her. To say, *when I knew her,*
is to say I knew something of what she dreamt
when she was young, *when she was young*
the circle skirt swept below her knees, is
to know something of her style, the gestures—
a flutter of hands. The distance intervenes.
How much is let go, what changes. . . .

The night I had the call someone had a vision
of a ballroom floating music over water.
Glenn Miller? Artie Shaw? And we walked
until the lights of the twilit boat appeared
and the music was carried over the water,
violet ripples, the turning sphere and click
slide of women slow-dancing in strapless

evening gowns, velvet masks, a world distant
from the slashed graffitied splendor of our
park. Distant as you are now, woman small
as a dancer, already half cold springtime

air, my last visit, the fierce consuming
cancer. The psychic's spinning globe
& the music of those dancing feet, your face

in April, lit with pain, & yes, apprehension
radiant above your hands' flying seraphim
attending to the sum & the glory & the flame.
Notes you'd send me pondered, stricken, composed
again on blue paper in your room with its
canopied bed, the desk with its garland
of lilies, casements opening to a garden.

To say, *I knew you*. The room empty
tonight, dust filtering its sloughed
transparent wings over the spines of books,
the neat half-moons of clipped fingernails
in a glazed dish by your bed. The ballroom
floats its melodies until it's spectral,
a radiant drifting to the insect's

furious orchestra, the waves, then gone.
From whence do we come, and whither
do we go—that ancient mystery.
A crystal globe spins its provinces, the city
where your room draws its veils. Beyond
the casements, the garden's iron gate
clicks open, and who is it now that enters?

At the Westland

*Life is in color, but black and white
is more real. —Sam Fuller*

The camera angle's high and dizzy:
    like a funneling throat, the elevator plunges
  down through the building.
Vertigo's intentional,
                landing after landing
  of whispering queens, flounce
of stained organdy, velvet. Like tropical birds.

Back in the room she shares with T.,
    zoom in on faces and moons
  in cracked plaster,
                fantastic rust continents.
The building's a hive the elevator cranks
  its tortured music through, its brass
and iron furbelows.

In the basement,
           the body waits to be found.
Spot of concrete, fish-eye view of sneaker,
laces untied, the ankle's
              unnatural splay.
Rose patterned scarf flagged from a beltloop.

It's clear this is just another
  wasted drifter. It's clear
we're in the realm of
the assailant's blind hammer, of chemical
    bliss that figure-eights to endlessness,

the camera impersonal
     as the rat's onyx-eyed regard.

From the basement apartment,
                         the Thai band
mangles the worst Rolling Stones, singer
     wrapping his supple body round the mike,
crooning *Angie, you beautiful,*
                         crooning

with no money in our coats, dark hair
     sweeping his lovely face, *you can't say*
we never tried. Tight close-up of the body's
hands,
       a bird exploding from silk.
                         The band's
dreadful machinery.
                    The elevator's cable spooling
down, down like an antique bathysphere,
latticed iron and brass.

Long pan of the street: hotels fizzing
     their names blue, green, rooming houses,
rundown apartment courts. Dress shopwindows where
     mannequins cock
     their taped and spavined wrists,

tulips shriveling petals to show black hearts,
     black hearts, the elevator going down.
     Pungent basement musk.

The pool of light its arrival throws
                            glimmers
Spider's good luck earring.
     Filtered, a glimpse
of the hammered face. Nothing pretty.
     T. saying *sweet Jesus, sweet Jesus,* while
she's flashing back through static swarming

air, the room mercuried
                         in dusk, pigeon loose
and flying frantic against walls, mirror,
chilly xylophone of hangers set ringing by
its wings.
          Static air.
                    Spider taking her scarf,
her blue rose scarf. Swarming buzz. The room's

     shades of rainwater, gunmetal, blue steel,
   the gasoline-on-water sheen
       of the bird's feathers.
The snared bird so hot and light, its furious
     heart. Like an omen. This orphaned dark,

ruined door of that face, and T. going
     I hope he was high, hope
   he was good and high.
Beneath the skin's thin veil,
                            her fragile bones.
   Skitter and distortion of bad guitar, the band's
machinery terrible, *all the dreams we held so close.*
The ankle's lifeless collapse,

that stacked feeling
of rooms above, hive of whispers, shrieks,
   slaps, moans of lovemaking, dust of the building's
slow decay.
         The saccharine lyrics,
                        tragic romance,
tragic sleep,
            a song she could not hear for years
after without remembering a hive — queens primping,
   addicts twitching out on their missions. The room
she shared with T. just after
      T. stopped modeling, faces and continents
   on the walls, the thin electric hum
of power feeding the Roxie's marquee,
         jazzing evenings maracaed by platform
heels trolling down the avenue.
                     The place from which

there is no shelter. The room they shared
   like the rooms in her mind
      the basement has joined, a hive,
the door already closing. She wants to learn
      to forget. Tinny music box chords.
Where will it lead us from here?
      The shattered face.

The cost.
      Looping through reels,
                  the infinite
figure-eights of film. The elevator cables'
   oiled thrum, the ride up,

     floor after black ceilinged floor, EXIT glowing
red, floor after floor.
                 Down the avenue, blackness
pools beneath parked and derelict cars,
  washes like mercury across the pavement.

From her figured scarf the bird
unfurls,
      silk and wing,
               in flight beyond the alley's
emptied suitcases,
    the buildings' opulent parapets.
She wants to give him that. Let him have that.

Bar Xanadu

A perfect veronica, invisible, scallops air
before the bull, the bartender's fluttering hands.
Tipped with silken fruit tinseled gold,
a dusty banderilla hangs above racked bottles,
burnt-orange. Your lacquered fingers streak
the cocktail napkin and the globe of cognac's

fragrant on the zinc bar. Fields of chamomile.
Close your eyes and then the night turns to coal
seamed with diamonds. Outside, a girl murmurs
her tired price, in pesetas, to passing men.
Irita, the barman calls when she wanders in
to wash at the single coldwater tap. Just a fly-blown

café on your functionary's street of flats, bedrooms
shuttered around their whispering, the shops that gleam
by day with scaled cellophane piglets, mounded bins
of fruit and olives. Irita rewinds her hair
at the bar, a gilt rosette nestling its waves,
tattered bullfight posters on the wall behind her

and you think of Rita Hayworth tossing roses
in *Blood and Sand*, the frayed banderilla.
Such a lovely thing to torture an animal with,
the corrida's exacting choreography
of life and death. Sometimes it's soothing to evaporate
in this smoke-patinaed air, abandoning

your imposter's life of embassy files breathing
the military names and numbers, Torrejón's
precise cold barracks. Your face wavers, oddly calm

in the mirror as the girl talks dancing and
flamenco clubs to the barman, absinthe glass shining
derangement in his hand. It's the place in the night

where you carve an uneasy confederacy
from vapor and exhaustion, a trio — the alien,
the clownish poseur, the girl with nothing to sell
but herself and straitened, cataleptic dreams.
She stretches, plays idly the slot machines
spinning roses, babies and lemons, the brilliant

suit of lights. The caramel glow of the barlamps haloes
her hair, bitten lips. Another sip and the slots'
click is rosary beads wafting prayers up
to a heaven of slink and spangle, quick bargains
struck in alcoves, that old palm of chapped fingers
slipping coins to the gas meter, of spreading stain

across the counterpane. Around Bar Xanadu
narrow streets fill with the violet steam
of after-midnight, the pigeons' soft venereal
cooing that speaks of want like this, that deep
original loneliness. There are heartless places
in every city you've lived. Cognac spreads

its window of warmth and the drifting years return
bordered with the crimes of night, with cramped
rooms you've climbed to, dead as the money
in your pockets. A "dimestore Mata Hari,"
the bureau chief called you while he snipped
a fresh cigar. On parched plains outside the city

soldier boys drill before the fighter planes, glamorous
with starlight, still floating half-sleep
in some Iowa of vinyl booths and Formica, miles
of hissing corn. But it's closing hour and beneath
your fingers the napkin snows its raddled lace
across the bar and you must rise with them, rise

to dust with the barman his green bottle, help him
to don the sparkling jacket. Rise to strap
the magic shoes to Irita's feet
and then you must walk with her these streets
you'll never leave, gritty with wind from Andalusia
riffling your skirt in the scent of blood oranges and sweat.

Fortunate Traveler

Dazed and voluptuous, Monroe sways through
    the casino towards Gable. The last film.
Her soft face, like her voice, breathless
    above subtitles, the Spanish premiere

    of *The Misfits*, thirty years late. The line had wound
the block beneath a sky, stagy
    and ultramarine, swept with klieg lights,
    sherried autumn air. Like a trapdoor opening

    in time, ladders and tunnels, the metro's
    black underground wind beneath the theater,
blue signal flash. Each platform's arched and tiled, columned
    and inscribed, resplendent as memory palaces

    monks once constructed, lavish scriptoriums
of the mind for arcane texts, scrolls and histories.
    I'd wanted to hear American voices, the velvet
    curtained hush framing spectacular faces.

Los Perdidos, the translation skews, the clement
    darkness violined as the stars navigate
tawdry celluloid orbits through the bungled script
    of drifters whose luck dissolves at desert's edge.

    Tossed dollar bills crisp around her ankles,
Monroe shimmies, the barroom scene, hair musical, those
    naked humid eyes. Houselights, dim, benevolent.
This morning, the Opera stop's electric

no-time, then the metro's plunge into the tunnel.
 Swaying from the handgrip on the way from
the doctor, his ancient fluoroscope that verdigrised
 everything it touched, my reflection rippled,

        insubstantial in the coal-blacked pane, tangled in
layers of reflection, circus posters tumbling
     half-naked spangled acrobats pentimentoed
 across the glass. Everyone I talk to these days

   is both here and not here, entranced by leaf-smoke,
        coal-smoke. Anthracite, the blue enduring flame.
Bituminous, yellow flame, burning quickly,
     volatile. Billowing tobacco clouds, the audience

   fans programs and onscreen the chemistry fails to
ignite but for this love scene, tender and confused,
      between Clift and Monroe. The alley outside the bar.
 They'd kept forgetting their lines, passing between takes

  a silver flask of vodka, washing down
       barbiturates until finally the shooting stopped
and that's why the scene's so lost. *Los Perdidos.*
    Crimson Seconals, the Tuinals and canary-yellow

  Nembutals, the stoked hues of leaves dervished in the parks'
dry fountains, sherried autumn air. Like trapdoors in time,
     a yeasty breeze redolent as the breeze shaking
  winged maples in the park by the railroad station,

the group of friends I had when I was young.
Another city. Of all that group, I alone
am left to glimpse beneath these actors' faces
other faces, behind Monroe's hand steadying

herself on the torn car seat this hand fluoroscoped
green and fleshless, all arthritic whorls and ratchets,
to see in those fanned bones the *transi*'s hand, caught
between life and afterlife, carved above

the sandstone archway in the ruined monastery
garden near our flat, already part of memory's
cluttered gallery. Here is the urn that holds
the lover's ashes, the harp that plays

the friend's delirium, the coal brazier measuring
time: anthracite burning blue, enduring, bituminous
sulfur flames, the quick ones, black-bordered postscripts,
those mistakes smudging police blotters. Of all that group

I'd meet when I was young: a trapdoor opening in time—
this one of the russet curls blown across a pale forehead,
this one I loved, rich laughter from a black throat like
no other, the spark and groan of trains braking at

the little station. Translation fails. The metro rumbles
beneath the theater as Los Perdidos reel suffused by
harsh mineral desert glow. When the last
shot of the actress's gone lovely face furls away,

I alone will taste the foreign coffee, sweet
        and thick. I alone shall watch these hands vanish
in bewildering autumnal smokes, an evening
        at this century's end when wrought-iron streetlamps

        print wands and serifs over everything
they suffer to touch.
        Of all that group I'd meet when I was young . . .
        I can't recall what we spoke of—it meant so much.

The Window

Streak of world blurred charcoal & scarlet, the El slows,
brakes near the platform, Little Chinatown,
& there's that window, peeling frame, screen split

to rippling raingusts. A curtain breathes
through busted glass, a glimpse of hallway
enameled green, rows of numbered doors, nothing more,

and then the train lurches forward sparkling
its electric signature above slick, hissing rails.
Soon, soon, I'll stop there, the window's pull

irresistible as the force of a star collapsed
to black gravity. I'll step through the window,
take up again the key for the one room to which

I keep returning. Let me wait again there by the sill
as I wait still. Here's the steeple of the burnt church,
beloved of vandals, the sooty block of

old law tenements where chipped tubs rise
porcelain on their feet in coldwater kitchens,
unashamed, small gray animals, the startled

array of insects we lived with.
Where are you? In the hallways, bodies passing
smell like bodies, unwashed, ginsoaked, dopesick,

the musk & salt. Where are you?
Hear with me the slant beat of that orthopedic shoe
striking pavement a few stained facades away.

With each echoing step, feel again the raw acceleration,
hope, or is it fear looming, receding?
Steaming hellmouths in the asphalt. If each of us

contains, within, humankind's totality, each possibility
then I have been so fractured, so multiple & dazzling
stepping toward myself through the room where

the New Year's dragon lies in its camphored sleep.
In the days I lived here, a thousand rooms
like it, making love was a way of saying *yes,*

I am here, these are my borders, hold me down
a little while. Make me real to myself. One more shining
thing gone after in the night that disappeared

with morning. No substance. But I'd like you
to place your hands, cradling the neck's swanny
arch, stand here by the copper dormer window

that's like an endless gallery of such windows
with fire escapes burdened by doves' insatiable
mourning. Then let it happen, the desire to be out

in the world, more than in it, wholly of it,
trammeled, broken to neoned figments.
All it takes is a few adjustments—

purple those lids, the lips as we did then,
that old mirror clouded with vague continents. We're
ready to inhabit the sequined gowns, martini glasses

pouring their potions over the street, the milky syringes
& oh, those ravening embraces, the ravished streets
& whispered intersections. Slick back

the hair, and then the wig. I could never face anything
without the wig. Transformed, the old vaudeville desire
struts & kicks its satiny legs, the desire to be

consumed by ruined marquees, these last drifting hotels,
to be riven, served up singing, arched & prismed
from a thousand damp boulevards. Those things which shine

in the night, but what vertigo to surrender, falling
through the elaborate winged buildings they only have
in neighborhoods like this anymore, January's bitten snow

cold about the ankles. Let me move again, a wraith,
past these windows—bridesmaids' gowns the color
of casket linings, flammable, green

as gasoline poured from the can to flame the alley
outside the Welfare's fluorescent offices,
police stations, the shabby public hospital's endless

waiting rooms. How exactly pinned-to-the-wall
love was in that harsh economy, the world, the world, the world.
What I remember is the astringent sting of air.

Living on nothing but injections & vodka, a little
sugar. The self, multiple, dazzling. What I remember
are the coral husks of lobsters broken clean

through restaurant windows, steaming. Through these
windows tumble fragments, the stories, lavish
vertical fountains of opera. Dressed as death's-heads,

crowds demonstrate against the new war
with placards before the marble stairs. Like a wraith
let me move among them, through the rooms

of this building, home of my fondest nightmares, let me
stay the hand twisting in rage, let me crush
the white & violet petals of sleep, the black sticky heart

of sleep over the delicate eyelids, over the bodies'
soft geographies, over the sorrow, the grandeur
of columns & esplanades, the soot-shouldered graces

outside the museum. Rude armfuls of orchids
fill the florist's windows, these lunar ones
curved like music staffs above dissolving aspirins

I might bring back to the room for you. Oh phantoms.
Oh the many lives that have fountained through
my own. Soon, soon, I shall stop upon that platform

& you will meet me there, the world rosegray beyond
the scalloped tops of buildings & we shall seek
that thing which shines & doth so much torment us.

Afterword

This volume gathers all of Lynda Hull's collections, including *Ghost Money* (1986), *Star Ledger* (1990), and *The Only World*, which appeared posthumously in 1995. A handful of unpublished and uncollected poems exist, mostly early efforts that were not included in *Ghost Money*. Because Lynda did not see fit to place them in either of the two volumes that were published during her lifetime, none of them appear in the present volume. At the time of her death in an auto accident in 1994, Lynda was planning to arrange into a new collection the poems that appear in *The Only World*, many of which had already been published in journals. It then fell to me to structure the book. As Lynda's husband of ten years, I was fortunate to have been the first to read and critique her poetry, and although the structure and selection of her last volume is not precisely that which I think Lynda would have envisioned, during the final months of her life I had numerous conversations with her about the arrangement and possible title for the collection that was emerging, and my organization for the *The Only World* attempts to reflect her wishes. The earliest poems in the present volume date from 1983; "Rivers into Seas," the last poem that Lynda completed, was finished a few weeks before her death. Lynda's individual collections have been unavailable for several years, and this Graywolf volume brings back into print the work of a writer of originality and depth, one of the finest poets of her generation.

Lynda Hull was born in Newark, New Jersey, in 1954, and experienced a fairly typical suburban childhood. At the age of sixteen, however, shortly after she had been awarded a scholarship to Princeton, she ran away from home. Her wanderings over the next ten years are charted in many of these poems, and they often make for unsettling reading. Because of an early marriage to an immigrant from Shanghai, she spent several of these years in various Chinatowns around the United States and Canada. I met Lynda in 1982, while I was teaching in Little Rock, Arkansas, and where she was living at the time. This was a relatively stable period in Lynda's life; she was pursuing an undergraduate degree (she would later receive graduate degrees from Johns Hopkins and Indiana University), had begun to work seriously on her poetry, and had for the first time in many years reconnected with her family, remaining close to them until the time of her death. We were married in 1984, and during our years together lived briefly in a number of locales in the United States and Europe: many of these places figure prominently in her poems. Our longest period of residence was in Chicago, where she composed most of *The Only World*.

An almost oxymoronic combination of elegance and danger, of lyric acuity and peril, characterizes Lynda Hull's poetry. Its elegance and rich lyricism derive above all from Hart Crane, her favorite poet. (Lynda at one point memorized *The Bridge* in its entirety.) The sense of danger and peril comes from her experience on the street, which scarred her in many ways. Yet her ability to survive those years also bestowed upon her an enduring sense of gratitude. The fundamental quality of her poems is compassion—both for the lost and disenfranchised souls who populate this book's pages and for the author herself as she looks back upon an often fraught and harrowing existence. They are grave and majestic poems, elegiac and celebratory at once as they confront what the ending of the poem "Red Velvet Jacket" calls "this world burning ruthless, crucial & exacting."

Thanks are due to the University of Iowa Press for permission to reprint the poems of *Star Ledger*, to Jeff Shotts and Fiona McCrae at Graywolf for their enthusiasm about this project, and to Lynda's family—her parents Christine and Eugene, and her siblings Chip, Christopher, and Mary—for their efforts at keeping Lynda's work and memory alive. And thanks are due above all to Mark Doty, whose unstinting dedication to Lynda's poetry, expressed so eloquently in his afterword to the original edition of *The Only World*, enabled this long overdue collected volume to be published.

—*David Wojahn*

Acknowledgments

Ghost Money was published by the University of Massachussetts Press (Amherst, 1986) as a winner of its Juniper Prize. Acknowledgment is made to the following publications where some of these poems appeared, sometimes in earlier versions:

Antioch Review 44, no. 2 (Spring 1986), "Maquillage," "The Bookkeeper," and "Little Elegies," copyright © 1986 by The Antioch Review, Inc.; *Crazyhorse*, "Accretion," "Arias, 1971," and "1933"; *Indiana Review*, "Preparing the Estate Sale" and "Remington"; *Missouri Review*, "Night Waitress"; *The New Yorker*, April 1, 1985, "Jackson Hotel"; *North American Review*, Fall 1984, "Autumn Mist"; *Poetry*, "Chinese New Year" and "Insect Life of Florida"; *Poetry Northwest*, "The Fitting"; *Sonora Review*, "Hollywood Jazz"; *Telescope* 3, no. 3, "Invisible Gestures"; and *Tendril*, "Tide of Voices."

"The Charmed Hour" and "Housekeeping Cottages" were included in *The Grolier Poetry Prize Annual* (1984).

"I would like to thank David Jauss, Elizabeth Spires, Denis Johnson, Richard Lyons, and all of my teachers in life whose care helped make this book possible. "Night Waitress" is for Maureen McCoy, "Remington" is for Richard and Maura, and "Diamonds" is for Yusef." —LH

Star Ledger was published by the University of Iowa Press (Iowa City, 1990) a winner of its Edwin Ford Piper Poetry Award. Acknowledgment is made to the following journals where certain of these poems first appeared: *Agni Review:* "Black Mare," "Magical Thinking," "Midnight Reports," "Visiting Hour"; *Boulevard:* "Gateway to Manhattan"; *Denver Quarterly:* "Fairy Tales: Steel Engravings"; *Gettysburg Review:* "Adagio"; *Indiana Review:* "Studies from

Life"; *Kenyon Review:* "Lost Fugue for Chet," "Carnival"; *Missouri Review:* "Counting in Chinese"; *New England Review/Bread Loaf Quarterly:* "Aubade"; *North American Review:* "Vita Brevis"; *Pequod:* "Frugal Repasts"; *Poetry:* "Shore Leave," "Utopia Parkway"; *Poetry Miscellany:* "Cubism, Barcelona"; *Provincetown Arts:* "The Real Movie, with Stars"; *Quarterly West:* "Utsuroi," "The Crossing, 1927." Several of these poems have also been included in anthologies: "'Black Mare" in *Under 35: The New Generation* (Doubleday); "Hospice" in *Poets for Life: Seventy-Six Poets Respond to AIDS* (Crown) and in *Pushcart Prize XV* (Pushcart Press); "Frugal Repasts," "Love Song during Riot with Many Voices," and "Shore Leave" in *New American Poets of the 90's* (David R. Godine).

"I would like to thank the National Endowment for the Arts for a Fellowship which allowed me to complete this book and the Yaddo and Edna St. Vincent Millay colonies for fruitful residencies. "Love Song during Riot with Many Voices" is for Dean Young and Cornelia Nixon; "The Real Movie, with Stars" is for Ralph Angel; "Adagio" is for Mark Doty; and "Abacus" is for soul-sister Barbara Anderson. "The Crossing, 1927" makes use of passages from Edna St. Vincent Millay's journals and is for Herbert Morris. "Utsuroi" owes a debt to Marina Warner. Most of all my best thanks to David, whose constant support and belief made this book possible." —LH

The Only World was published by HarperCollins (New York, 1995). Acknowledgment is made to the following journals, in which these poems first appeared: *The American Voice:* "Chiffon"; *Colorado Review:* "Red Velvet Jacket"; *Crazyhorse:* "Rivers into Seas," "Denouement"; *Denver Quarterly:* "River Bridge"; *The Iowa Review:* "Fortunate Traveler," "Amulets"; *Indiana Review:* "Bar Xanadu," "Street of Crocodiles"; *The Kenyon Review:* "Suite for Emily"; *New England Review:* "Fiat Lux"; *Ploughshares:* "Ornithology"; *Pushcart Prize XIX: Best of the Small Presses:* "Suite for Emily"; *Red Brick Review:* "At the Westland"; *Third Coast:* "For Ann." Thanks are also due to the National Endowment for the Arts and the Illinois Arts Council for fellowships that aided the completion of this collection.

Collected Poems has been typeset in Berling, a font design by Karl-Erik Forsberg in 1951 for the Berlingska Stilgjuteriet in Sweden. Book design by Wendy Holdman, composition by Prism Publishing Center, and manufactured by Versa Press on acid-free paper.